Trash Fish

TRASH
FISH
A Life

by Greg Keeler

COUNTERPOINT BERKELEY

Library of Congress Cataloging-in-Publication Data
Keeler, Greg.
Trash fish / Greg Keeler.
p. cm.
ISBN-13: 978-1-58243-402-5
ISBN-10: 1-58243-402-6
I. Title.
PS3561.E339Z46 2008
813'.54—dc22
[B]
2008013093
1-58243-402-6
978-1-58243-402-5

Cover design by Anita van de Ven
Interior design by David Bullen
Printed in the United States of America

Counterpoint
2117 Fourth Street
Suite D
Berkeley, CA 94710
www.counterpointpress.com

Distributed by Publishers Group West

1 2 3 4 5 6 7 8 9 10

For Judy Keeler

"This isn't half the story."

Part I

My mother is a fish.

Vardaman in Faulkner's *As I Lay Dying*

Long Lake

When I was a toddler, Father tied me to the seat of our rented rowboat. That was around 1950 on Long Lake in Minnesota. I know there are probably at least as many Long Lakes in Minnesota as there are Trail Creeks in the West, but this one was just a morning's drive from the Twin Cities, where he was working on a Ph.D. in American studies. He tied me to the seat because the first time he took me out, I scared the shit out of him, which might seem fairly unlikely since he was a two-hundred-pound-plus Hemingway scholar and I was a fifty-pound ball of ADHD. Anyway, here's how it went:

"Hey, Fargle, your bobber just went under."

"Gottabite! Gottabite! Gottabite."

"Take it easy. You don't have to stand up."

"Gottabite! Gottabite! Gottabite."

"Stay in the bow, son. You don't want to . . ."

"Gottafish! Gottafish! Gottafish!"

"Yes, that's a nice sunfish, but you're going to . . ."

"Get 'im! Get 'im!"

"Get back in the Goddamned bow!"

"Bawwwwww, got away. Bawwhoohoo!"

So we baled out the boat, and for rest of the weekend Father rowed this tether-ball around to the coves and inlets of Long Lake, and bouncing in the limits of my clothesline rope, I caught a dozen or so fat sunfish.

In the ensuing years, I sometimes found it difficult to understand why Father chose to go fishing by himself half the time. After all, he liked to fish, I liked to fish and I was his son. But now, looking back, it's not quite such a mystery. Fishing with me must have been something like bird-watching with a cat. As soon as we'd pull up to a stream or lake, I'd be out of the car, dashing toward the lake, falling over boulders, spilling the tackle box and falling in the water. Father would stand by the car trunk muttering under his breath, knowing that nothing short of violence could stop me; then eventually, he'd come after me, picking up hooks and sinkers in my wake and finally rigging up his own rod.

Not that he was any great shakes himself. His equipment was always frayed and clogged from use and abuse. His casting reel sometimes looked like a porcupine with all the loose ends poking out from where he'd knotted the line together after cutting out backlashes; his rod was short and stubby from breaking and regluing the tip so many times; and his lures— they were huge old concoctions of metal, feathers and wood, resembling small rats or squashed pigeons. But probably, if I learned anything specific from my father about the process of angling, it was how to swear. After all, when one lets one's tackle become a huge tangled wad, one has a bit of trouble turning it into anything but found art. One of my earliest vivid memories is of Father standing out on a point of rocks on Lake Skaneateles in upstate New York, silhouetted against a fuchsia sunset, jumping up and down, screaming "Fuck, fuck, fuck." I can't remember if it was over faulty equipment, a lost fish, or life in general. All I remember is the "fuck" part.

When a reel got a backlash in it, in Father's hands it ceased being a plain old reel and became a "jacked-off-spool-of-horse-fuck" reel. Once in Oklahoma when he was pulling a stringer of small bass from a farm pond and a water moccasin had managed to work one of the bass into its gullet, it ceased being a water moccasin and became the "bastard son of an elongated turd." And once when he was cleaning a channel cat and his hand slipped so that its dorsal spine went into his wrist, it ceased being a channel cat and became a "scum-sucking, mucus-drenched nail in the hand of Jesus Christ Almighty."

There was also violence. If he broke the tip of a rod, sometimes, instead of replacing the tip, he would take what was left and break it again in several places. It isn't easy to break a fishing rod in several places. Sometimes one must find a couple of cinder blocks so that one may lay it between them and stomp it. Or sometimes one must just rear back and send it whoop-whooping out to the middle of the river. For the most part, Father was a gentle man, but fishing was, for him, a sort of ventilation shaft through which raged the sound and fury of his simian predecessors.

Fish Currency

. . . .

But aside from the bondage, stomping and profanity—or maybe in no small part because of them—these early memories were enough to establish an addiction, so much so that the imagery became part of my earliest dreams. In the subliminal zone, the sunfish on Long Lake became, on the one hand, a sort of bright currency, coins and jewels flashing their turquoise, orange, red and green up through the Freudian murk of my early childhood. And as I've grown older, they've left the water and I'll go on surreal fishing trips, tossing my baits and gaudy lures behind the furniture of my bedroom or under the trees and hedges of our backyard, and catch huge fantastic creatures that swim the air until I pull them close enough to be terrified and wake up. I suppose the lawn and bedroom fishing were as much a product of my waking experiences as of my unconscious. Sometimes after hard rains on my grandfather's farm in Oklahoma, he and I would walk the grassy pasture behind his house and find catfish trying to swim the wet grass between ponds. Once he picked up a three-pound channel cat wriggling behind a prickly pear cactus. We had it for dinner that day. To me it tasted more like rabbit than fish.

Sometimes the dream-fishing-turned-nightmare still follows me in my adulthood, where I catch fish that rot as soon as I pull them from the water, or I'll be surf casting and giant ocean fish that I witnessed on the early TV series *Crunch and Des* or the movie *The Old Man and the Sea* will take my bait and drag me screaming, as if on water skis, out to the deep water, as afraid to hold on as I am to let go. And still, as a dream-toddler, I'll walk out the front door of the Quonset hut where my family lived in Minneapolis while my father went to graduate school and hear an eerie gargling, wailing noise. When I look down into the puddle before me, it's a small fish with my mother's head pleading with me. I never have any idea of what she's saying. I only know that I'm responsible.

But don't take this too seriously. I sure don't. No sir, I'm one healthy, well-adjusted guy. We all leave our miniaturized mothers gargling and screaming in puddles at one time or another.

Roadkill Bonanza

Perhaps I should wade out of this dream-water for a while toward something a little more rational and positive—say, my grandfather. Ah yes, Granddad, my mother's father, now there's someone who would never shrink and scream at me from a puddle. Maybe we'd both shrink and scream at someone else from a puddle, but at least we'd be in it together. Had Granddad been in that boat on Long Lake with me instead of my father, he probably wouldn't have tied me to the seat. More likely, he would have joined me in my ecstatic lurchings until we capsized. We were an odd couple, a pink, coddled English professor's son and a leathery retired wheat farmer, but we both had an obsession with fish that bordered on the unhealthy.

In the early fifties, when he'd take me fishing in his battered, dust-clogged '36 Chevy, replete with a backseat full of gunny-sacks to hold the catfish we caught, I learned to be ready for episodes like the following:

A young jackrabbit runs out in front of us and pings off of the front bumper. As I watch it pinwheel in the rearview, Granddad's eyes light up, like he's just spotted a bag of money. He skids to a stop, jumps out, grabs it by the hind feet, whangs its head against the back fender, tosses it on the gunnysacks behind us, gets in and heads for the nearest farm pond. As I turn around and stare at it, bug-eyed and quivering in its death throes, I'm hoping that this thing won't wind up on the dinner table this afternoon, so I venture the question.

"What's the rabbit for?"

"What's that, Bub?"

"The rabbit, what's it for?"

"Don't you know what a rabbit's for?"

"No."

"Same thing these are for, but better." He pats the Ball jar next to him, still warm with its contents, the guts of a freshly killed hen.

"Bait?"

"Bait."

When we get to the pond, he unrolls the trotlines from their coffee cans. To Granddad, these trotlines are finely honed tools on which he sharpens the one to two dozen hooks every evening before he goes fishing. Soon he has skinned the rabbit and cut its flesh into half-inch cubes, which we pop onto the hooks. Then he takes a stake at one end of the line, I take one at the other, we stretch it across the deepest corner of the pond and we shove the stakes into the mud. While we wait for trotline action, we take some chicken guts and toss them in the shallow water near shore. In less than a minute, several huge crawdads coalesce out of the murk, and we reach out and grab a couple behind by the back with our thumbs and forefingers, so that they flip their tails and wave their ominous claws about, until we pull off their tails and throw their front halves out on the pond. We then untie the cane poles from the roof of Granddad's Chevy, bait them up with the fresh tails, toss our corks out and wait.

All these little killings, guttings and beheadings were a bit surprising to me, but they never seemed brutal. They just seemed like a part of Granddad, who more often than not carried a slight smell of fish and blood along with the usual cigar smoke. Hitting a wounded rabbit's head against a fender or tree or wringing the neck of a downed duck or quail was as much a part of his outdoor ritual as sharpening his hooks or cleaning and polishing his shotgun.

On one of the rare occasions when my father (who never hunted) went hunting with me, I shot a quail and he, obviously distressed, walked over to where it was fluttering and flopping in the wheat stubble.

"Jesus Christ," he said, "it's still alive. Shoot it again, quick."

"Why?" I said. A product of Granddad's ethics, I had no idea why Father would be upset or why he would want me to waste another shotgun shell.

"It's suffering," he said.

"Not for long," I said. When I walked over to the bird and pulled off its head, my father started to cry. Seeing my father like this, I would have cried too, had I not been twelve years old and a hardened product of playground bullying. I knew that Father had been a lieutenant on a destroyer that had survived a direct hit by a kamikaze, so I figured that the crying must have been over something other than the little head clutched in one of my hands or the little body dangling from the other. Back then, I had no idea how much Granddad resented Father for stealing Mother, his only child and his best friend, or how Father was growing to resent Granddad for stealing me.

Damn, I'm starting to make shit up so I'll sound deep. Back to the pond.

After about ten minutes of watching our corks bob over their crawdad gobs, some swirls begin to appear where we've set the trotline, so Granddad unstakes one end and picks it up to expose three bullhead catfish and the head of a huge snapping turtle.

"Let's get that turtle off," says Granddad. "Lift the other end." So I pull up the stake on my end, and we drag the fish and turtle to the bank. While the giant turtle hisses, gacks, and scrabbles, he opens his jackknife, saws off its head, and casually frisbees the body out over the pond. It goes whop when it hits the water and hasn't yet sunk as he returns to unhooking the mudcats and tossing them into a wet gunnysack.

After a few hours, the gunnysack sags with several flopping pounds when I lift it from the water, so we chug and bump back over a few miles of red dirt road to the farm, where we throw the wet sack of writhing fish down in the chicken yard and go up to the house and get Grandma to clean them. Yes, that's right, I said we go up to the house and get Grandma to clean them. I have to repeat that because I have trouble myself believing that such a thing happened. Grandma is another story.

Grandma, Chickens,
Cats and Guts

. . . .

She loved to fish. She loved to eat fish. She loved to clean fish. When she couldn't go with us, she would always be ready to ooh and ah over the visceral mass Granddad dumped from the gunnysack, and then she'd gut, skin and behead them with relish. The imagery is still clear. She's surrounded by farm cats and hens, poised for their share of the kill. The shadow of her bonnet bobs around a fat mudcat as she takes her kitchen knife and cuts a circle around its head. Then, clamping the slick skin in her pliers, she pulls it off like a wet sock and flings it out into the yard, where chickens tear it from one another's beaks or a cat dashes out and chokes the whole thing down. By the time she's worked her way through the half dozen or so fish, the chickens and cats have retreated to various corners, squawking and hissing at each other, trailing guts, skins and heads.

The next day, the fish are on the table. They've been soaked in brine overnight, dipped in flour and cooked in hot lard, and they taste like the Lord Jesus himself came down and cooked them. I say that because Grandma always had to attribute the fish to the Lord Jesus, even though we all knew that they came from a muddy pond looking like something a big cat threw up, and it was Grandma alone who had transformed them into something that, to me, tasted like the proverbial chicken, though Grandma's preferred standard was channel catfish, and when she'd prepared chicken she'd say, "Don't this chicken taste just like channel cat?"

Fishing with Grandma was also something else. She and

I would usually dispense with distances and drive out to the
pond in the pasture behind the house. Since the trotlines were
Granddad's territory, we'd just sit on the bank with our cane
poles fishing with chicken guts.

Grandma knew a lot about chicken guts. Many times I'd
watch the process through which she would arrive at the guts:
the chasing, the grabbing, the pathetic walk to the stump, the
chopping, the headless torso running in bloody circles, the
scalding, the plucking, the mysterious inversion of the gizzard,
and ultimately the guts themselves.

Greg and
Grandma Noir

Grandma Noir: Where are the guts?

Greg: I left them in the car.

Grandma Noir: I told you, the guts are your job today. Your
only job.

Greg: I'm sorry. I'll get them.

Grandma Noir: Your only job.

*Greg (fetching jar of guts and holding them out to Grandma
Noir):* Here are the guts.

Grandma Noir: Bait your own hook today.

Greg: But . . .

Grandma Noir: Bait your own hook today.

Greg: OK *(Greg puts a string of guts on his hook with his six-year-
old head turned to the side)*

Grandma Noir: What goes around a button?

Greg: Thread?

Grandma Noir: No, a goat.

Greg: I don't understand.

Grandma Noir: You know, a goat goes around a button.

Greg: How can that be possible?

Grandma Noir: I guess you're just about as smart as your dad.

Greg: I guess.

Grandma Noir: You've got a bite.

Greg: I can't see my cork.

Grandma Noir: Yes, it's under the water. Pull.

Greg: There's nothing there.

Grandma: You missed her.

Greg: Why?

Grandma Noir: You waited too long.

Greg: Look, your cork is gone now.

Grandma Noir: (jerks her pole from horizontal to vertical in less than a second, and a large mudcat sails by, knocking her flowered bonnet off and landing in the grass behind them) She's a fat one. I didn't know we had any fish that fat in here.

Greg: Why?

Grandma Noir: Why what?

Greg: Why's she so fat?

Grandma Noir: Because she has eggs in her.

Greg: Why?

Grandma Noir: You ask too many questions.

Greg: Why?

Grandma Noir: Go get the gunnysack.

Greg: Why?

Grandma Noir: Do you want me to go get the strap?

Greg: Why?

Grandma: I'm going to get the strap.

Greg: Why?

Gut Bucket
Reminiscences

. . . .

Because Grandma and Granddad raised my mother during the Depression, they were accustomed to killing birds, animals and fish every which way to keep themselves and my mother fed. Once when things were exceptionally tough, Granddad went out to the granary where a mass of grackles had accumulated on the rafters, lifted his shotgun and blew down a dozen or so with one shot. Mom said as far as she could remember, they tasted okay considering the alternatives.

And once in the middle of a particularly awful winter, Grandma spotted a covey of quail scooting around in a huddled clump under the big fir tree near the outhouse. With unlikely stealth for such a large woman, she scooted right up behind them, whomped a gutbucket over the whole clump and, one by one, whisked them out and beheaded them. Granddad said they ate like royalty for a week.

Long after the Depression, my grandparents still had an instinct for seeing our furred and feathered friends around the farm as meat. Though jackrabbits weren't usually the desired fare because of their toughness and their propensity for carrying parasites, Grandma was once smitten with an insatiable craving for rabbit. Between Granddad, the coyotes and the hawks, most of the cottontails had been culled out that year, so Granddad and I headed for the back pasture to "doe-pop a jack or two." I find the following scene particularly memorable because I never heard him say "fuck" before or since.

"Granddad, over there, a jackrabbit—and it looks like it's hugging another jackrabbit."

"Where?"

"Over there by the gully, see 'em? What are they doin'?"

"They're fucking." *Boom.*

"You shot them."

"Two in one. Not bad, eh, Boliver?"

"You shot them."

"Yes, I did. And they're young ones. Should be tender."

Watermelon, Popcorn and a Two-Dimensional Possum

. . . .

I mention these various attempts by my Oklahoma kin to pro-
cure culinary wonders through questionable methods in order
to set the stage for my cousins, Ralph and Leo. They were
Grandma's sister's sons, who lived in their mother's tarpaper
house on the Salt Fork River. When Ralph was a toddler, he
had fallen off the porch of that house and onto a piece of glass,
so that he was half paralyzed and still walked with great difficulty, even at sixty when I knew him. Leo had tried marriage,
work, business and the military but wasn't that fond of any of
them, so he returned to Ralph and the tarpaper house on the
river.

Now, considering my post-*Deliverance* perspective, I might
be a little more guarded about those visits to Ralph and Leo,
what with their overalls, their union suits with drop flaps, their
dental incongruities and Ralph's propensity for yodeling when
he talked. But as a child, I felt like Granddad and I were visiting
magicians as they emerged pale and blinking from the tarpaper
darkness, pulling up their suspenders and offering fresh pop-
corn and watermelon from their patch out back.

Eating watermelon with Ralph and Leo was an experience
in itself. When it had been a modest watermelon year, Leo

would cut them with a knife and we would try to conduct dialogue between swallowing and seed spitting.

Ralph would lower a slice from his mouth with his good hand and get the conversation rolling with something to the effect of, "Nnggoodhuhngpatooi."

"How's the, *schlorp gulp*, wheat this year. *Foooof . . . ting*."

"Looked like it was gonna get forty (*gackahack*) bushel till that hail hit, *schlomp*."

"This sure is good. *Gurk, hoof hoof hoof . . . .*"

"Go easy there, Boliver. Don't choke yourself."

On better years, when melons abounded, Leo would dispense with the knife and crack them open on a log, the steps, his knee—whatever was most expedient. We would also dispense with dialogue—and with the hindrance of seeds, choosing rather to dig the hearts out with our hands, eat them like apples, and throw the rest to the ubiquitous chickens.

Once the watermelon was out of the way, we would enter my cousins' profligate realm of fish gathering. Granddad would bid me to fetch whatever roadkill we might have found on the trip to the river from its bed of gunnysacks in the back of the Chevy. The freshness of the kill wasn't crucial to Ralph and Leo. In fact, something that had baked and flattened in the road for a day or two would frequently be more suited to their purposes. A flat possum was usually easier to tie to the mesh at the bottom of their fish trap than a three-dimensional one. And the local catfish that had acquired more sophisticated tastes preferred one that exuded a certain piquancy and perhaps even a few maggots.

That the trap approximated the size and shape of a coffin lent a macabre element to the process, especially when combined with the image of Leo's pale skin turning slightly blue after he stripped and eased into the chilly water to situate the device. Because the two brothers had long since abandoned fishing poles for their lack of efficiency, we were, on occasion, hard-pressed to find entertainment while waiting for prey to seek out the submerged carrion. Sometimes Granddad would bring his .22, and he and Leo would take turns blowing the heads off turtles where they sunned themselves on distant logs, and sometimes Ralph would regale me with woodland lore, such as the tale of the large water moccasin he had seen choking down a duck or the saga of the twenty-pound carp he had harpooned single-handedly with his pitchfork.

And I, pressed by youth and inexperience, would concoct colossal lies of my own streamside derring-do. I would tell them how I packed a cherry bomb into a ball of Wonder Bread and, after chumming the water with crusts, threw the ball into the feeding frenzy and how, after the explosion, I caught the raining sunfish in my baseball mitt. I would tell them how, during thunderstorms, I could hold my Zebco spin-casting reel to my ear and pick up radio stations in Mexico. During my lies, Granddad and Leo would look off into the trees and blush, but Ralph would hang on every word, sometimes lending approval and validation with, "I seen dynamite do the same thing," or "I heard a fella talkin' French when I took the fence out back in my teeth."

Then, toward late afternoon, we would all haul at the rope tied to the front of the trap until we saw dark shapes moving and then heard the frantic flopping of large catfish.

There were other occasions when Ralph and Leo would tire of such primitive methods and resort to twentieth-century technology. On such occasions, the fish trap would lie dormant, high and dry on the bank, and they would head for the large pools the river left when it receded during dry weather. They would, as Leo put it, "phone up a few."

Though it employed cutting-edge technology, it was a rather simple process. Ralph would kneel at one end of the pool, cranking furiously on the handle of a country telephone generator, a device common in farmhouses of that period, and

Leo would kneel at the other end of the pool, cranking furiously on the handle of another telephone generator. Soon the surface of the pool would be aquiver with its occupants, the furious cranking would stop and the dip netting would start.

Peleg Goes Fishing

When I was seven, my mind was sufficiently developed to decide that Father didn't take me fishing enough. The year before, we had moved to Cortland, New York, for Father's first full-time job in the English Department at Cortland State Teachers' College. That's right, Cortland, New York, home of Cortland fishing line, Cortland reels, Cortland you-name-it. My father certainly went fishing enough. I'd watch him return home from sojourns to the Tioghnioga, the Onondaga or Factory Brook with messes of whitefish, smallmouth bass and brook trout. I'd sit in our backyard knocking hazelnuts off the trees or squishing elderberries between my fingers, waiting to see what he'd bring home next so that, like mother, I could ooh and ah and perhaps win him over for the next fishing trip, but no dice.

In desperation I finally came up with a plan. I wandered upstairs to his study, where he was finishing his dissertation on American grassroots democracy. He glanced up from *For Whom the Bell Tolls*, puzzled that I wasn't planted in front of the television and *Superman*.

"I love you," I said. Father gave me a look like some creature had just moved inside his stomach. I figured he must not have heard me right, so I repeated it with a different emphasis.

"I love you . . . Dad." Mouthing something I had heard my mother say in one of her frequent moments of emotional candor, I added, "I just figured that people don't say that enough to each other and that the world would be, well, a better place if they did."

He put down *For Whom the Bell Tolls*, wandered over to his

bookcase, pulled down his copy of *Death Comes to the Archbishop*, opened it and started thumbing through it, as if it might contain some profound rejoinder. Then he looked up and said, "OK, Peleg, I'll take you fishing."

I thought he had called me Peleg Greg because, several years before, I had quite publicly peed myself when I found the Minneapolis Zoo to be lacking in restroom facilities. I didn't know at the time that he called me that because Peleg was one of the Quaker owners of the Pequod in *Moby Dick* AND because I had quite publicly peed myself.

All in all, the nomenclature didn't much matter because, after that, he started to include me in his fishing forays. When he was sneaking up on little pools of brook trout, I would come clattering down the bank, dislodging rocks and trailing brambles, to ask if he could perhaps spare a worm. When he was pensively reclined against a tree, watching his bobber and musing on Henry Nash Smith's *The Virgin Land*, I would come shrieking out from behind a boulder, covered with ants. At his wit's end, he finally came up with a way to keep me occupied. He showed me how to catch chub.

Yes, he would find a slow, oozing tributary, bait up my little outfit and put me on a pocket of chub. In this way, I learned how to catch and unhook fish and to re-bait because I was constantly catching fish. Skill and patience went out the window, and chub came flopping in. Because chub taste something like an inner tube pickled in sewage, Father discouraged me from honing my fish-cleaning skills on them, but he did let me keep them. He gave me a big jar, which I filled with stream water and kept beside me as I fished. Thus our fishing trips turned into true quality time. Father could relax and consider profound comparisons between Thoreau's *Walden* and the panoramas that stretched before us, and I could watch the multicolored chub convex and plink against the walls of their jar as it became more and more crowded. Before we went home, I would always release the chub back into the element from whence they came—though most of them would just sort of bob away, belly up.

My Cortland experiences only amplified the obsessions I developed for the magic of fish as a toddler on Long Lake, Minnesota. Otter Creek flowed right next to our yard, shallow enough to assuage my parents' fears about my drowning but deep enough to harbor crawdads and the occasional trout. I knew nothing about the latter until one day when the city drained the creek. I remember wandering down the bed in awe and reverence, finding small brook trout flipping and churning in the shallow pools, somehow reminding me of Mother's jewelry.

On another occasion, the city stocked the creek with brown trout, and some local civic group sponsored a fishing contest. I hadn't yet developed the facility for catching trout, but I remember wandering across the bridge near our yard slack-jawed as I watched older boys walk by with willow twigs loaded with the marvelous creatures. I also remember a young man in an ill-fitting game warden outfit offering assistance to boys who had just caught fish.

"That's certainly a nice one, son."

"Gee, Mister, ain't he swell?"

"You shouldn't let him suffer."

"What?"

"You shouldn't let him suffer. Here, let me break his neck."

"But . . ."

Snap.

Then the young man was off to the next kid down the stream, leaving the previous one staring at the limp, crooked shape in his hand.

"That's a good one. I think it's a female."

"How do you know, sir?"

"Because she's more rounded and has a smaller lower jaw. You shouldn't let her suffer. Here, let me see her."

"Why?"

Snap.

Etc.

The magic continued when the family made weekend excursions to Skaneateles, one of the nearby Finger Lakes where our next-door neighbors, the Booths, had a cabin. The trip there was always a bit harrowing because the steep, downhill, dirt road from the highway to the lake was filled with hairpin curves verging on vast drop-offs. Father would go *arnk, arnk* when we'd hit bumps and be briefly airborne in our pre-seatbelt Ford. On one of the last curves, when the fear was beginning to wane, we'd pass a shack where two hermits lived. They would frequently run out to our car, reeking of booze and God knows what else, and Father, who had a soft spot for the down and out, would engage them in brief conversation while Mother hung her head out the passenger's window, gasping for air.

"Where ya headed?" they'd ask from the stubble and stink of their beards.

I'd think, *Fishing. Let me out of here.*

But Father would say something like, "To hell eventually," or "To the nut house if that sonofabitching Eisenhower has a say in it."

Then, with the smell of boozy laughter in our car, we'd descend to water so pure you could drink it straight. When we rowed out on it, huge boulders bulged up from the depths, and we'd lower our minnows twenty or thirty feet down where rock bass would take them, and we'd pull them flopping into the boat, where their red eyes would shine like Martian Jujubes.

A Two-Lane Dream

. . . .

Did I mention, in all of this talk about, well, me, that I have a brother, Ted, who is a year and a half older than I am? While I spent much of my youth engaging the flora and fauna, Ted was more inclined toward the meditative and analytical side of things. Starting at five, he would memorize railroad timetables, road maps and world geography. I remember some evenings when we were lying on our bunk beds in Cortland, he would grill me on state capitals just to keep me on my toes. And well before that in Minnesota, when on weekends I would argue for a drive in the country, Ted would argue for a trip to the train station where we would watch the locomotives, massive embodiments of his predictions in time and space, chuff to and fro.

I also remember two specific times when our worlds intersected and we went fishing together. One took place in Oklahoma during the summer of 1956. It was a trip with Granddad to Art and Rosie Rose's pond, which was just a mile or two from his own place. It is easy to remember Art, because he never bathed and "fuck" was a major part of his everyday vocabulary. When we stopped by his farmhouse to ask how the fishing had been recently, he said something like, "I found several fucking nice ones up in the fucking pasture after that last fucking rain." I don't know about Ted, but Art and Rosie were such kind people that my mind short-circuits when it tries to connect Art with his smell, his language and the large fish we caught on his place.

When we arrived at the pond, it was definitely high and muddier than usual, and it was jammed with crawdads. I recall wondering, when Granddad had us bait up with crawdads, how it would be possible for the fish to find ours among all the others—but they did. I have a distinct memory of Ted's cork, which was actually made of cork, moving across the surface of the pond and Granddad saying, "It's probably just another big crawdad pulling it," but Ted jerked anyway and it was a huge mudcat. Right after that, my cork did the same thing, and I caught one too. Around that time, Ted was teaching himself to take and develop photographs, and he took a picture of me, scowling into the sun with my hefty mudcat.

I also remember a fishing trip during the spring of that same year in Virgil, New York, a small town near Cortland where our family lived for two years before we moved back to Oklahoma. Our grandparents had given us English bicycles for Christmas, so we pedaled into the surrounding hills, fishing among the marsh marigolds for pickerel and then in the clear pond near a schoolmate's house for whatever might be swimming there. I think we only caught a few chub that day, but they were colorful, and their color became part of that spring with its budding trees and its two-lane highway that still carries me and my brother in my dreams.

Since then our paths have separated according to our interests. While I was doing my best to follow in various family footsteps—fishing, hunting, chasing frogs and crawdads or swearing, Ted was honing his skills at photography, conducting experiments with his chemistry set, writing short stories, learning astronomy and studying the geography that stretched far and away toward Reed, then Harvard, then MIT and, by his early thirties, the vice chairmanship of the Economics Department at Berkeley.

Our Lady
of Jackass Flats

. . . .

So far I've said very little concerning Father's side of my family,
perhaps because, except for Father, there wasn't much fishing going on, and perhaps because there was just too much
tragedy involved. Granddad Keeler, a country doctor, had Par-
kinson's disease when I was an infant and died soon after, his
brother was cursed with a humpback and Granddad Keeler's
daughter, Father's sister Margaret, died at twenty-five. Before
she died, however, she bore a daughter, also Margaret, and
this Margaret, though she was several years my senior, was the
focus of my first major crush. Raised by Grandma Keeler (yet
another Margaret), in the house in Lamont, Oklahoma, where
Father had been raised (a house where God was pronounced
"Gawd" in hushed reverence), she carried enough magic with
her to balance any absence of fish. Her sharp wit and kind
manners pulled me bouncing along behind her, investigating
the hummingbirds and large yellow and black striped spiders
in Mother Margaret's garden, collecting a large jar of cicada or
locust shells that we plucked from the trunks of locust trees
or peeking in on the huge toads that occupied the dilapidated
root cellar.

I must have been nine or so when she broke my heart. Of
course, she had no idea that she had broken my heart. Hell,
I had no idea that she had broken my heart. Mother Margaret had sent her from her house in Lamont out to my fishing grandparents' farm a few miles away because she and her
boyfriend, Bill, were getting too close. There, she was to have

a cooling-down spell and transfer her hormonal angst over to a day of bucolic bliss with her aunt's mother (Grandma Noir) and her young cousin, Greg.

I was in heaven, thinking that I would have this magical being all to myself for a day of boysenberry picking and witty repartee. Duh. How could I have fathomed the reason why any question or suggestion that I or Grandma proposed would be met with uncontrollable sobbing?

"You might as well get used to it. You're here for the day," said Grandma.

Shriek.

"Why don't you play with Greg? He's been waiting for you all morning."

Shriek.

"Would you like to see the big sunfish I'm keeping in the cattle tank?" said Greg.

Shriek.

"Or how about we pick boysenberries? There are tons of ripe ones," said Greg.

Shriek.

"You be good to your cousin. You'll have a much better time with him than you would with that young man in town," said Grandma.

Shrieeeeeeeeeek.

Now, after half a century and a tumultuous life as an Okie in California, Cousin Margaret has returned to Oklahoma, where she has a little place near Luther on some land once owned by Ralph and Leo. In the spirit of all that wit and passion, which still make her dear to me, she calls her place Jackass Flats and occasionally lets me fish there—even though the pond contains no fish.

What's on the Bottom

. . . .

Just before my early adolescence, my family moved from New York back to Stillwater, Oklahoma, where I was born. Father taught English, and Mother eventually taught home economics at the college there, while Ted toyed with the universe and I pedaled my bike furiously between school, home and the creeks and ponds surrounding us.

One of my favorite spots was Theta pond, an elaborate landscape ornament bordering the college campus and hemmed in by old stone walls, gravel walkways and park benches. As I grew older, I learned that, in myth, its bed was lined with rubber, condoms discarded from late-night trysts on the surrounding benches. But as a kid, I needed no myths to appreciate the bullheads and sunfish that drifted below the surface among the moss and duck poop. During the summer, my friend Scott Daggett and I would coast down the gravel paths armed with hand lines and Wonder Bread. Scott's granddad had convinced us that dough balls were superior to any other bait. We knew he must have had some expertise in the use of grains because he caught huge carp by tying hardened cakes of cottonseed meal and flour bristling with hooks to trotlines and setting them on Lake Carl Blackwell, the local reservoir. We hadn't yet advanced to the stage of mixing cottonseed meal and flour, so we just rolled up balls of Wonder Bread and crammed them on treble hooks. Without rods and reels, the going was a little tough, but neither of us knew the difference as, hand over hand, we retrieved the occasional sunfish and bullhead—at least until I met James.

In the fifties, Stillwater was a fairly typical Southern town when it came to race. Black people and white people pretty much ignored each other, and the black people always got the short end of the stick. I didn't see many black kids fishing on Theta pond, but when I did, they were usually by themselves. One July when Scott had been dragged off to church camp, I was fishing by myself and saw a tall, skinny black kid about my age and shape fishing across the pond with a rod and reel. That alone piqued my interest, but when he pulled in a huge bullhead and then threw it back, I had to wander over and make inquiries.

"What you using?"

"I'm using chicken guts."

"Where'd you get 'em?"

"I got them from a chicken."

"That's a nice outfit you got there."

"Yes, it's a South Bend. They're having a sale on them down at Murphy's Hardware."

"How much?"

"Three dollars and fifty cents."

"How 'bout the rod?"

"The rod was included."

"Why'd you throw it back?"

"Throw what back?"

"That fish."

"Good Lord, who would eat those things? Just look at this water, the scum and duck crap, and Lord knows what's on the bottom."

"I guess you're right." I thought about how I'd been eating these fish for a month; then I thought about Granddad once saying, "Niggers'll eat anything, turtles, carp—no matter where they come from."

"My name's Greg. What's yours?"

"James."

So James and I spent the afternoon fishing together. James's color wasn't the only difference between him and the other boys I'd met in Stillwater. He spoke clearly and in complete sentences, something like my brother. I was intrigued.

My parents had always tried to show racial tolerance around me, though for Oklahoma in the fifties, that wasn't saying much. I remember seeing Lena Horne on a television variety show and Mother saying, "My, she's a handsome negress," and Father saying, "Yes, she certainly is." I could tell that they were trying to demonstrate some kind of tolerance, though, even at the time, I knew there was something twisted about the word "negress," and I never saw them dashing down to the shacks on the southeast side of town to make friends—even though some of those shacks were quite spiffy compared to the one where my cousins, Ralph and Leo, lived.

The next afternoon, I showed up at Theta pond with a new bargain basement South Bend rod and reel, which I had afforded only through a furtive raid on Father's change tray. As James patiently showed me how to use it, I realized that much of the tolerance in this equation would most likely come from him.

Neither of us talked much about our backgrounds except for our granddads and fishing, and the more we talked, the more our granddads sounded like the same person—the way they dressed, the ways they fished, the types of cars they drove. One evening in late July, James's granddad came down to the pond to see why James was late for dinner, and I saw that he even looked like my own granddad.

"Come on, Jim," said James's granddad. "You're late for dinner."

"I'm sorry. I was talking with my friend here," said James.

"What's your friend's name?" said James's granddad.

"This is Greg," said James.

"I think it's time to say goodbye to Greg," said James's granddad.

And I never saw James again.

Family Relations and Child Development

Now that I could go fishing on my own, I practiced and improved on the techniques Father and my grandparents had taught me. Of Father's contributions, I suppose the abuse of equipment and language figures most prominently into these early days of independence.

I was fascinated by closed-faced spin-casting reels, which were just coming into vogue in the late fifties. Some resembled shiny green insects, some had swooping contours and fins resembling the Chrysler products of the time and some were plated with blinding chrome and resembled cheap jewelry. All were simple to abuse and, in no time at all, became the objects of my most inventive profanity. I recall a particular reel that I spotted in one of the many sporting catalogs that I ordered through *Field and Stream*. With a thumb piece shaped like fins at the rear and housing as sleek as a rocket ship, it became my obsession.

I even had an elaborate dream in which the reel possessed supernatural powers. I put it on a long golden rod and took it to my sixth-grade class at Eugene Field Middle School, where girls whom I had secretly admired gathered around to touch it. At home, when I was putting it back into its box, it conversed with me.

Reel: I have traveled far to find you, my son.
Greg: But I bought you from a catalog. I don't understand.

Reel: Out of millions, I have chosen you and only you to do
    my bidding.
Greg: You mean like casting and stuff?
Reel: That and so much more. Have you not seen how the
    young women look at me?
Greg: You mean girls?
Reel: Ah, you are such a child. Remove my housing and
    observe the mysteries of my inner workings.
Greg (embarrassed): I think you'd better go back in your box.
Reel: Put me back now, and I shall never speak again.
Greg: But will I still be able to fish with you?
Reel: Only when you are wading in the shallows.
Greg: I guess that will do. *(puts reel back in box)*

I must have worked for two weeks, gathering pecans in a
nearby grove and lugging them to the owner's house, where
she paid me fifteen cents a pound, and then another week
working at a local greenhouse for a dime an hour until I was
fired for over-watering and killing a roomful of geraniums. But
finally, I had enough money to order the reel. When I removed
it from its box, it lacked the charisma of the one pictured in
the catalog, but it still looked enough like a small rocket ship
to impress my friends.

After being stepped on and driven into the mud, dropped
on the road and ridden over by a buddy's bicycle, left out in the
yard and urinated on by a German shepherd and taken apart
and put back together wrong, it lasted about a month. By the
end of that month, I had become frustrated with the reel and
was in our backyard trying to cast with it, but it only made sort
of a whing-ding noise, and owing to the many knots and kinks
in the line and the reel's cattywhompus innards, I could only
fling my casting plug about ten feet before it popped against
the end of its tether and came bouncing back at me. When
Mother entered the backyard to investigate the commotion,

she found me on my knees, pounding the reel flat between two pieces of cinderblock and trying to improve on Father's lexicon of expletives. Because she had recently been boning up on family relations and child development for her classes at the college, she felt compelled to explore the situation.

"Gregory, is that the new reel you worked so hard for?"

"Yes."

"Is there something bothering you? Something besides the reel? Maybe something at school, or maybe your dad or Ted or I did something?"

"No."

"You mean it's just the reel?"

"Yes."

"Are you sure you don't want to talk about it?"

"It's just the reel, Mother."

"Just the reel?"

"Yes, Mother, it's not school, it's not Father, it's not Ted, it's not you. It's just the reel." And, for all I knew, I was telling the truth.

Whatever Works

. . . .

The farm ponds around Stillwater were nothing like the ones sixty miles northwest near my grandparents' farm. The ponds up there lay in depressions among wheat fields that flattened toward the horizon. They were almost always muddy and full of catfish. The ones near Stillwater lay among hills of scrub oak and sandstone and were usually clear and full of bass and sunfish, with the occasional channel cat. Both types harbored massive bullfrogs that went *harunk, harunk*, and were rumored to eat, among other things, their young, mice, and tarantulas, but for the most part, the ponds bore little resemblance to each other.

Fishing for bass and sunfish in these clear waters was a new and mysterious process. When my friends and I saw monstrous bass on the cover of *Field and Stream*, phantasmagoric plugs were usually dangling from the huge black holes of their mouths. And when we'd pedal down to Murphy's Hardware, we could usually find the same plugs, which looked even more impressive than they did on the page, sporting names like Hula Popper, Jitterbug, Devil's Horse, Tiny Torpedo, Lucky Thirteen and Chugger Ike. The only problem was that when I'd scrape together a couple of weeks' allowance to buy one, a faulty reel would fling it into oblivion, or I'd break it off in the willow branches above Lennigar's Lake or Overholt's Pond. Only occasionally would a small, unfortunate bass impale itself on a treble hook. And when my line didn't break and I managed to keep a lure for any period of time, one of the giant *harunking* bull frogs would stop *harunking* when it saw the plug chugging and sputtering along, swim out to it and try to eat it.

After a while, my family tired of frog legs, and frankly, there is something rather awful about hooking and retrieving bull-frogs. They're so anthropomorphic with their little forelegs and little frog fingers. Catching them, dispatching them and reliev-ing them of their hind legs was an exercise in the grotesque that left me with no shortage of imagery for my nightmares. I wondered how I had come to run so far afoul of the myth in my quest for the noble bass. This was not *Field and Stream*.

I bared my soul on this subject to Mr. Frazier, who managed the sports section at Murphy's, and he pointed to a little bin of tiny lures with fat, brightly colored heads, rubber legs, feather hackles and huge eyes.

"You tried poppers?"

"Poppers?"

"Yeah, these things." He held one up and wiggled its little legs. "Bass love 'em, bluegill love 'em, and if one of them frogs comes after it, you can whip it out of the way."

Soon it was all poppers for me and my friends—big pop-pers, little poppers, poppers with feathers, poppers with legs. We even started ordering popper components from catalogs and making our own, gluing the cork or Styrofoam bodies to the humped shanks of popper hooks, painting them, souping them up like hot rods, and decking them out with tiger stripes or flames down their sides. Frantically flailing and whipping them around at the end of my spin-casting rod, I had a whee of a time and toted home many a sunfish and small bass for Mother to ooh and ah at as I skidded to a stop in our driveway, stringer swinging from the handlebars of my bike.

But there was still a problem. I had to get close to smarter, bigger bass because I couldn't cast poppers very far. With my present equipment, I had to madly whip them around just to fling them twenty feet, and with all of the whipping and fling-ing, larger bass would go sploosh and flee in horror, leaving massive wakes in the moss.

So back to Mr. Frazier I went, wild with stories of sploosh-ing bass and giant wakes, and he said, "You mean you aren't using a fly rod?"

"No, why would I?"

Mr. Frazier shook his head and said, "No particular reason. You go ahead, keep scaring those big fellas with your little Zebco outfit," and he turned to help another customer.

When I got home, I rummaged through our storage shed and found Father's old bamboo fly rod. He had never learned to use it, but once in a while he would take it out, put it together, shake it and speak in a soft voice about rarified mountain water and trout fishing. The tip was missing from the time I used it to poke a badminton birdie out of a tree, so I found the tip of a deceased casting rod in Father's tackle box, glued it on, threaded the ancient line through the guides, tied a pop-per on to the frayed and kinked leader, went to the backyard, wrapped myself in line and hooked the popper in the back of my head.

Undaunted, I went to the library the next day and read up on fly casting. I forget the name of the book I lit on, but it espoused the virtues of the English casting method and poo-pooed the American method. Using the former, one mustn't bring one's rod back any farther behind one than twelve o'clock; using the latter, you cast as far as you can any which way you can. Perhaps because Father was an English professor or perhaps because I fell under the spell of the author's snob-bery, I went with the English method, and after another week or so of wrapping myself up and hooking myself, I became proficient enough to go back to Murphy's and buy a cheap, solid fiberglass fly rod.

"Changed your mind, huh?" said Mr. Frazier.

"Whatever works," I said.

"You're going to play hell learning to use that thing," said Mr. Frazier.

"Are you an aficionado of the English method?" I asked, whipping the rod to twelve o'clock above me with one hand and holding out a ten spot with the other.

"Jesus Christ," said Mr. Frazier.

God's Country

Picture Greg casting his poppers in the English style on a small lake in South Dakota, where his family is visiting his aunt and uncle who live in the nearby town of Lead. Greg's uncle, his father's brother Elon, has previously taken Greg and his father to several small lakes in the area, and Greg has caught so many trout on flies and poppers that he has become smug and self-satisfied. On this particular lake, however, in Custer State Park, Greg has caught no trout, but he has caught many of the same species of small sunfish so common in his home state of Oklahoma. He has just removed a longear sunfish from a popper when a barrel-chested man with a beard, a mustache and a hat worn in the style of Theodore Roosevelt's Rough Riders approaches him. The man's face reminds Greg of Ernest Hemingway, whom he has seen on the covers of his father's novels.

"You will only catch small sunfish here," says the man. "Sometimes after the hatchery trucks come, you will catch rainbow trout, but their noses will be blunt and their fins will be worn from the hatchery tanks. They will not fight well."

"Oh," says Greg.

"Where did you learn to cast like that?" says the man.

"From a book," says Greg. "It's the English style. You only bring your rod back to twelve . . ."

"Yes, I know, to twelve o'clock," says the man. "It is an effeminate style. It will not serve you well in a country of stronger fish and bigger water."

"Oh," says Greg.

"Where are you from?" says the man.

"Oklahoma," says Greg.

"That is worse than Iowa," says the man.

"What do you mean?" says Greg.

"You come here to the American West, following the hatchery trucks and laying trout like firewood into your coolers of dry ice."

"Oh, no, sir," says Greg, "I only catch enough to . . ."

But the man does not seem to be listening to Greg.

"Have you ever been to Montana?" says the man, gazing at distant pine trees.

"No," says Greg, "but I've ordered flies from Dan Bailey's, and they're . . ."

"Montana is nothing like this state with its little mud puddles and its slums of trout," says the man. "Montana is God's country."

Greg tries to imagine a country that God would designate as his own, but lately he has been having trouble imagining God at all, much less his country.

"Oh," says Greg.

"A man could do worse than live in Montana," says the man. Suddenly he reaches for Greg's fly rod and removes it gently yet forcefully from Greg's hands. "Let me see your little perch pole. Here's how a *man* casts." He whoops the rod way back past twelve o'clock and simultaneously hauls at the line so that when he releases it, it shoots sixty or seventy feet out on the lake, where a tiny sunfish immediately blorps at the popper.

"Gawd," says the man, handing the rod back to Greg, "I loathe this place."

Greg had been feeling pretty good until this man arrived. He had liked the way the pine trees made the air smell. He had liked the clear water. He had liked the cold trout with their bright colors and tiny scales—no matter where they came from. So Greg says, "It's not really all that bad."

The man looks at Greg as if he were a dog caught pilfering

from a trashcan. "Yes, well, what with Oklahoma and all. But in Montana," he reaches down, picks up a large, flat, half-submerged stone and turns it over, "in Montana's Madison River, the bottom of this stone would be crawling with life—stone fly, May fly, salmon fly nymphs—more than a man could count."

Greg wants to say, "What about a woman?" thinking of his grandmother, but instead he says, "I think I hear my mother calling."

"If you opened a trout's stomach, you'd find more species of aquatic fauna than there are in this whole state. And the Yellowstone," says the man, "the Yellowstone is even richer. I remember one hatch when you couldn't even see the river for all the caddis. If a man put his fly out there, it would have to go through three layers of caddis flies to find water."

"My mother . . ." says Greg.

"Here," says the man, frowning at the rock in his hand, "here you might find a snail if you're lucky," but the man is talking to himself because Greg has left.

Balloons of Questionable Meat

Much of my soul is still stuck in the mud of Oklahoma, far below all this talk of English casting and Montana, back in the primordial ooze with my totem spirits: trash fish. Even before Oklahoma, I remember an experience on Long Lake that approached the mystical. Our rowboat was bobbing by the dock where Father was untying me from my seat, when a motorboat sputtered up beside us, and two men got out carrying a golden glowing fish of such dimensions that its tail touched the dock. I can only hint at the dialogue between me and Father that must have accompanied the original perception of such an image.

"Whazzat?!"

"It's a carp, Greghorse."

"I wanna get one. Let's go back."

"No, son, you can't eat carp. They're dirty—yucky."

"They're keeping that one. Let's go back. I want one."

But we didn't go back, and it wasn't until a few years later, when Granddad and I were sitting on the banks of the Pond Creek River near Lamont, Oklahoma, that his cane pole flexed and he lugged a huge carp flopping and whopping to the bank.

"Can we keep it? Can we, huh, huh?"

"She'll eat."

"Boy oh boy. She's a beauty."

"There'll be bones. Lots of 'em."

"Will it taste yucky?"

"Not out of here, Bub, the Pond Creek has good water, and your grandma knows what to do." And it did taste pretty good, though the next day at the table, Father, Mother and Ted only ate catfish while Granddad, Grandma and I gacked and hacked on carp bones.

In Stillwater, my irrational carp worship continued when I'd bring them dripping into the house from forays to nearby Stillwater creek. Mother would humor me with some forced oohing and ahing, but I could tell her heart wasn't in it— especially when I put a small one in the aquarium in our living room, where it sucked and rooted in the gravel and gobbled the small worms I dug in our yard. It caused quite a stir at English Department functions. I still hadn't caught on to the fact that many didn't share my enthusiasm as I stood entranced before the aquarium watching the golden scales flash under the fluorescent light.

Even into my high school years, I managed to cling to my fantasies that carp might be something more than balloons of questionable meat and tiny bones, so one night, after my friends and I had driven out to Lake Carl Blackwell and fished with dough balls while we smoked Swisher Sweets cigars and talked about girls into the wee hours, I brought two pretty, shiny, river carp suckers home and cleaned them. The next day, seeing how attractive the well-cleaned torsos looked, there in their shallow pan of chilled salt water, Mother was deluded into cooking them. She showered them with dill, decked them out in lemon slices and popped them in the oven. They had looked so beautiful, like some delicacy out of *Ladies' Home Journal*, that we had trouble believing our senses when the kitchen started to smell like vomit.

One would think such episodes might have dissuaded me from my illusions concerning trash fish, but as an alcoholic eventually returns to drink after some horrid morning when he says, "Never again," so I eventually returned to my totem spirit.

In the early seventies, as a graduate student in Pocatello, Idaho, I smoked up a bunch of chub with Dr. Smith, my landlord and Renaissance professor, and the next day we couldn't tell if they had been smoked or if they had rotted. During the same period, I studied up on the pickling process, caught a mess of handsome suckers out of the crystalline waters of Johnny Drink Springs where it runs into the Portneuf near American Falls Reservoir and cautiously let them pickle for weeks in Ball jars in the basement of my friends Jennifer and Ed. When, bursting with anticipation, I finally removed one of the lids, ready to receive the culinary accolades of my friends, it was like opening a manhole cover on raw sewage.

But that didn't stop me. Once, when the trout weren't biting on the Snake River where it pours out under American Falls, I became mesmerized, gazing down from the bluffs into the deep water where massive carp and sucker hovered like zeppelins, and I uncontrollably fell to digging worms with my bare hands, baiting up and hauling the giants in. After I had several of them there on the bank with me, all of us panting and heaving in the evening sun, I didn't know what to do, so I found a big tattered pillow case in the back of my VW bug convertible, squeezed them into it, and lugged them to Dr. Smith, who said, "Those are really nice ones, Greg. Why don't you take this shovel and bury them out in our vegetable garden?"

In the mid-seventies, when my wife, Judy, and I moved from Pocatello to my first full-time teaching job at the university in Natchitoches, Louisiana, I was tickled pink to find a pond near the university, a pond full of bass. And giant goldfish. The former provided hours of entertainment between classes and office hours, but as I wandered the banks of the pond casting Krazy Krawlers or Shannon Twin Spins, my attention would always drift from the bass to the giant orange shapes drifting lazily a few feet below the surface. Local lore had it that the keepers of a nearby hatchery used regular-sized goldfish for bass food and that many had escaped and grown into these colossal carp in drag.

I tried dough balls, worms, corn; I even tried to snag them, but nothing doing. In desperation, I went to DeBileux's (locally and prophetically pronounced "Dubya's") Hardware and bought a barbed arrow and a bow-fishing reel, which I duct-taped to my old archery bow. The black men and women who regularly populated the banks of the pond, jerking out the occasional bullhead and sunfish with their cane poles, showed obvious amusement at the tall, skinny professor, sneaking around behind the willows and pausing to launch his tethered arrow into the murky depths.

Drawn by curiosity, an older woman finally approached me.

"What you doin', son?"

"I'm trying to shoot one of these big goldfish."

"Ohhh, I see," she said, and returned to her friends farther up the bank, where there was a general murmur of what I construed to be approval. After a few days, I finally connected with one and hauled it gasping to the shore, where it writhed on the grass and bled profusely where the head of the arrow protruded. I was stunned by its freakish beauty, bulging huge and golden in the sun, but horrified by what I'd done. I was standing there feeling like I had just skewered a big pretty pet when a crisply dressed black man walked up beside me.

"Looks like you got one."

"Yes, isn't it pretty?"

"She sure is."

When he said "she," I was even more horrified because now I not only felt that I had impaled a big pretty pet but that I had also impaled a big pretty female, so I said, "I feel kind of bad about shooting her. It's not like I can release her back into the water."

"Well," said the man, "don't you want to eat her?"

"You mean you can eat them?"

"Ohhh, yeah," he said, "she'll eat," and I felt like I was again in the presence of Granddad, even though he had died a decade before.

"Do you want her?"

"You mean you don't?"

"Not if you do."

"It's a deal," said the man. "What's your name?"

"I'm Greg."

"Well, Greg, I'm Reverend Willie Varnum, and you have my permission not to feel bad about what you done. In fact, son, I'm blessin' you here and now."

I didn't want to tell Willie about symbols or epiphanies or thematic significance for fear he'd see me for what I was: a young white professor who didn't know his ass from a hole in the ground. But the next day, I felt honored when I saw the reverend stalking the bank with a new bow, fishing reel and barbed arrow.

Ten years later on a brief visit to England, I was pleasantly surprised to discover a whole culture devoted to trash fish. In a move of predictable civility, the English say "coarse" instead of "trash"; thus, as I was taunting pigeons under Admiral Nelson at Trafalgar Square, I glanced at a magazine stand and saw *The Coarse Fishing Mail*. Inside were photos of English anglers clutching pig-like carp to their tweed bosoms. I was also delighted to see several unfamiliar species streaking their sports jackets with mucus—tench, barbel, loach—all to be tossed in huge live holding nets so they might be released and caught again by ardent Brits using elaborate chum catapults and long fiberglass bait-casting rods. Later, I felt a vast tradition welling up around me as I watched denizens of the sceptered isle haul shiny meat balloons from the Thames, the Serpentine and the lake in Regents' Park.

Many of these trash fish reveries culminated in the recent past when I went out on the upper Missouri here in Montana, where I have lived for the past thirty years, and fly-fished for carp with Andrew Steketee and our guide friend, John Talbot. We saw many of the huge creatures, some of which were waggling their tails in the shallows. John called these active ones "happy carp" and showed me how to cast crayfish imitations to them, but I didn't catch any. They were too smart.

Thirty-Five Steps to Arriving at Sheer Horror on Lake Tenkiller

After my high school friends and I learned to drive, we commandeered our parents' cars and, having tired of fishing Stillwater Creek, Lake Carl Blackwell and the many ponds dotting the local countryside, careened toward the eastern hills of Oklahoma, where Lake Tenkiller backs up many clear blue miles of the Illinois River. There in the foothills of the Ozarks, we grappled with our adolescent hubris and feigned adulthood in rented motorboats and ill-fated camping trips. Here follows a brief instruction manual garnered from such excursions.

1. Ask to borrow parents' new car for trip.
2. Borrow parents' aging Nash Rambler.
3. Pack sleeping bags, frying pan, fishing rods, dough bait, lures and Coleman lantern.
4. Stop at grocery store for Twinkies, paper plates, plastic knives and forks, grape pop and lard.
5. Drive east.
6. When radio doesn't work, make up obscene lyrics to Beatles tunes.
7. Break down.
8. Cut off frayed end of radiator hose with jackknife and jam less frayed remnant into place.
9. Fill radiator with muddy water from ditch with rusted can found in same ditch.

10. Arrive at lake and tell friend, "Sure, I'll swim out to the island with you."
11. Because you don't know how to swim, tie Clorox bottles to thumbs to stay afloat.
12. Halfway out to island, turn back because thumbs are becoming big and purple.
13. Panic and kick so hard that cutoffs trail from ankle.
14. Encounter Girl Scout troop on shore.
15. Pretend they are only laughing at your thumbs.
16. Replace cutoffs.
17. Suggest boat rental to friend.
18. Go to Six-Shooter Docks and rent motorboat.
19. Argue about why dock is named Six-Shooter and lake is named Tenkiller.
20. Sputter out to island in dark, still arguing.
21. Arrive at island tired and exhausted.
22. Try to light Coleman lantern in dark.
23. Fail to light Coleman lantern in dark.
24. Try to catch fish for dinner in dark.
25. Fail to catch fish for dinner in dark.
26. Eat Twinkies in dark.
27. Try again to light Coleman lantern in dark.
28. Discover Coleman lantern needs fuel.
29. As friend tries to fill Coleman lantern with fuel, say, "Here, let me light a match so you can see."
30. Ignite fuel.
31. Burn friend's leg.
32. Throw fishing, cooking and camping gear back in boat.
33. Help burned friend into boat.
34. Sputter back to Six-Shooter Docks, then drive frantically to emergency room.
35. Spend night lying next to friend on boards of dock while friend moans in pain.

An Iraqi's Lackey

After my brother finished high school and fled Stillwater to Reed, then Harvard and then MIT to give his mind a run for its money, I stayed in Stillwater for my B.A. and then my M.A., with a brief stint in Turkey with the Peace Corps between. As long as my mind could dwell on fish, it didn't particularly care where it was. In junior high math, I drew a bar graph literally of marlins to illustrate the difference in size and weight between species. In high school I wrote papers on commercial and sport fishing and oceanography. In art I made tile mosaics of a bass and a giant angelfish.

When, as a senior in high school, I learned that there was a building at Oklahoma State (which was by then a university) devoted to something called aquatic biology, I was ecstatic. I immediately tried to get a job at the lab, a small mysterious building on the west side of the campus. I figured my chances were pretty good since the head of the lab, Dr. Doris, had two sons who were my classmates in high school. When I went in to inquire, I felt as if I had walked into a dream. The place smelled like fish, ponds and formaldehyde. A huge live alligator gar loomed in a tank before me. Sunfish and bass gleamed from their aquariums. Pickled on a shelf, an exotic paddlefish lay curled in a giant jar, and fat little daphnia bounced in their fish bowls, soon to be fed to the surrounding fish.

"How old are you, son?" said Dr. Doris, stretching behind his desk in the front office and gazing out a window.

"Seventeen, sir."

"What are you planning to major in?"

"This, sir."

"You can't major in this. You can major in zoology or fish and wildlife."

"OK, sir."

"OK, what?"

"OK. I'll major in one of those things, sir."

Dr. Doris shook his head. "Tell you what, son, you come back when you're actually majoring in one of those things, and we'll talk about a job."

So that summer, with gar and daphnia swimming in my head, I took a job as a janitor in a girls' dorm where, dreaming of the gar tank, I stood in the basement by a pile of Kotexes, tampons and God knows what else at the end of a chute where trash fed in from ten floors, shoveling it all into a raging incinerator.

That fall, I took some requisite freshman classes and paid special attention to biology so I could drop by Dr. Doris's lab occasionally, hang around the gar tank and make small talk about biological stuff in hopes of upping my chances for a job that summer. It worked.

Off and on for the next few years, I tagged along after graduate students out in the field, doing titrations on farm ponds, seining small streams and backwaters, putting along on Keystone Reservoir between Stillwater and Tulsa and shocking fish from a Boston Whaler with booms and electrodes hanging off the front, learning to use weird scientific devices like Eckman dredges and Kemerer bottles, weighing and measuring fish and taking scale samples—generally getting paid a dollar an hour to do what I would have paid at least as much to do.

My favorite of the grad students was Tarik Al-Rawi, an Iraqi working on a doctorate in fisheries biology. I had known of him from the pre-job days I spent hanging around the gar tank because Dr. Doris had once yelled, "Where's that God-damned Arab?" and another graduate student had explained that Dr. Doris's dismay stemmed from the fact that Tarik played fast and loose with lab equipment. Ultimately, Tarik hoped to return to Baghdad and use his doctoral experience to improve fish populations in the Tigris and the Euphrates Rivers.

Tarik had an obsession with fish that may well have surpassed my own, so barriers of language and culture fell away like water in the wake of our Boston Whaler. Tarik would recite the species of each fish stunned with our shocking equipment, weigh it, measure it, take a scale sample and return it to the water, while I jotted the numbers on a data sheet. I could tell he delighted in handling the fish, and his Iraqi accent made each name into a ritual mantra:

Bloogeel: seven point five ounces, eight eenches. Splash.
Cotfeesh: one pound, foorrteen ounces, feefteen eenches.
    Splash.
Carrlp: thrree pounds, seventeen point five eenches.
    Splash.
Bahhs: fourr pounds, thrree ounces, twenty eenches.
Shod: fourrr oonces, seeks eenches. Splash.
Etc. Splash.

Another graduate student, Steve, a Southern Baptist, was as unimpressed with Tarik's pronunciations as he was impressed with my unbelievable naiveté, so one day in the lab he asked me, "Do you know what Tarik's religion is?"

"No, I never really thought about it."

"He's from the Middle East, isn't he?"

"Yeah, I guess."

"You know, I'll just bet he's a Jew."

"Could be," I said, plinking my finger against the side of the gar tank, trying to make the big guy move.

"Why don't you ask him?"

"OK," I said. Tarik being Jewish made sense to my blank-slate brain because his humor and demeanor reminded me a little of my Jewish friend, Neal Gladstone, who had taught me to play the guitar. I should also mention here that the Yom Kippur War was raging at the time, and Tarik was keeping close tabs on the battles, listening to his transistor radio as we bobbed around on Lake Keystone. But my blank-slate brain convinced me that he was just a diligent follower of current events.

So during lunch at the Kopper Kettle Kafe on a hill where the county had moved the town of Keystone after they built the reservoir, I said to Tarik between bites of pecan pie, "Are you, well, Jewish?"

"What?"

"Jewish—are you a Jew?"

Some of Tarik's coffee came out of his nose, but after a while he was able to talk. "No, Greg, I am not a Joo. I am what you might call the opposite of a Joo. Why ees eet that you are asking me thees question?"

"Steve wanted to know, so I told him I'd ask you."

"Ohhh, I seee," said Tarik. "Well, maybe you cood ask Steeve a leetle question for me."

"Sure," I said.

"Perhaps you might ask heem why eet ees that hees face bears such a close resemblance to the buttocks of a peeg."

"It sort of does, doesn't it?" I said, feeling a small corner of my blank-slate brain start to fill with the rudiments of an essential truth.

"Yes," said Tarik, "eet sort of does."

Tarik and I became friends after that, and somehow friendship allowed us to do really stupid things in front of each other—like the time Tarik pushed a large fish trap from the boat but forgot to tie it up to its rope and marker, so he jumped in after it, wallet, watch, and all. Or the time Tarik backed the trailer up to the boat ramp, and instead of shoving the boat off the trailer, I unhitched the trailer and safety chain and

watched the tail light wires snap as the whole enchilada went
rolling into the lake. Dr. Doris eventually had to amend his
expression of dismay to "Where's that Goddamned Iraqi and
his Goddamned lackey?"

Because Tarik and I both became so agitated when in the
presence of a big fish, we sometimes put our lives in peril, as
when a huge bass once came boiling up between the electrodes. It was usually our credo as scientists to let fish go after
we had our statistical way with them, but sometimes Tarik
couldn't bear to part with a particularly big and beautiful bass.
This time, he was at the controls, and I was up front with the
dip net.

"Look, look! Eet ees beeg feesh! Get heem, get heem!"

"Where? I don't see him. Over here?"

"No, no, not there, the other side. Queek, he ees seenk-
ing."

Tarik left the controls, came charging to the front of the
boat, grabbed the net and leaned out, but the boat hit a rock so
that he lost his balance and started to topple between the humming electrodes. I immediately hurled myself into the back of
the boat against the generator controls, shutting it down just
as he hit the water. Or maybe it was the other way around.
Maybe I got excited, dashed to the front of the boat and started
to topple, and maybe Tarik lunged for the controls. I've told
it both ways so many times, I forget which is the truth. You've
read about me up to this point, so you be the judge.

At any rate, twenty-five years later, when America started
bombing Baghdad and then again a decade after that, I felt
horribly complicit and wanted to hunt down one Bush or the
other, grab him by his little shoulders and scream into his
smug little face, "I thought you liked to FISH!!"

An Ignorant Island

"Rolled 'Round in Earth's Diurnal Course"

Wordsworth

. . . .

When I wasn't out with Tarik, tinkering with death, Dr. Doris would sometimes send me to work with Rex, a small, pleasant-mannered doctoral candidate, who was already a rising star in limnology, or the study of lakes. Rex also worked on Keystone, and his experiments required that his Boston Whaler have a huge motor so that he could speed back and forth across the lake, taking oxygen samples and chemical titrations at speci-fied points to determine how light and temperature at different times of the day and night affected the chemical structure of the lake. Experts in the field had dubbed these frantic twenty-four-hour data-gathering sprees "diurnals."

No fish were involved in these gambits, so I had to take my pleasure in the cool clarity of the water we'd draw up in Kemmerer bottles from deep in the lake or the slight fear that pierces one as one races across water on a moonless summer night at four thirty in the morning, trying to get to the next sampling station before dawn. Over the howl of a wide-open throttle and the slamming of the bow against whitecaps, Rex would sometimes try to explain what we were doing.

"OK, Greg, let me make it simple."

Rowwwrrrrrrrowwwrrrrrrowww.

"In meromictic lakes . . ." *Bamwhambamwham.*

Bamwhamwhamwham . . . "but with an inversion" *. . . Bam-whamwhamwham.*

"There are lakes with two basic types of structures."

Rowrrrr. Bamwhamwham. Whambamrowrrrr.

"Chemoclines . . ."

Bambambam.

"And thermoclines."

Whamwhamwham.

"Understand?"

Rowwwrrrrrowwwrrrrrrowww.

"Understand?"

Whambambambambam.

"Greg?"

Rowwwrrrowrrrrr.

Because Rex's research was on the cutting edge of the field, Dr. Doris took special pride in his work and would occasionally accompany his bright protégé on these diurnals. In the dark depths of the night on one such trip, Rex and Dr. Doris were *whamming* and *bamming* bleary-eyed across the lake when an island interrupted their research. The island didn't know much about chemoclines or thermoclines. The island didn't know much about anything. As Rex and Dr. Doris went whizzing across the tops of its shrubs, then clunking over its rocks, and then coming to a rest in a clump of its boulders, it didn't even notice the difference in the pitch of the motor as it went from *rowwwrrrrrowwwrrrr* to *wheeeeeeeeeeeee*.

After Rex and Dr. Doris made it through this diurnal with only a bruise or two, Tarik, over coffee at the Kopper Kettle Kafe, felt at liberty to make a little joke at their expense.

"Perhaps the two of them peed themselves een the trauma of the moment."

"It's always possible."

"So, Greg, what would yoo call their boat under these circumstances?"

"I give up."

"A di-urinal."

Egor, Lothar and Renfield

. . . .

I have always appreciated Mary Shelley's *Frankenstein* as a lesson in the hazards of science run amuck, but it wasn't until I participated in several Gothic experiments that I truly understood what horrors might be perpetrated by well-intentioned biologists.

It was only after two years of working for Dr. Doris and the aquatic biology lab that I was allowed into a more secretive, darker realm of the natural sciences known as the Oklahoma State Cooperative Fisheries Unit. I won't taint the name of the professor who supervised this unit. He was not responsible for the horrors that transpired, so let us, for thematic convenience, call him Dr. Frankenstein, and let us call the graduate students who worked under him Egor, Lothar and Renfield —and, of course, there was I, Gregor, the henchman to the henchmen.

My hovering spirit still lies mute, motionless and aghast on a particular arm of Lake Keystone where one of these grisly episodes unfolded. Egor and I were to treat one hundred square yards of that arm with rotenone, a compound that would deplete the designated area of oxygen and kill a select number of fish so that we could make a thorough and accurate study of the population in that area. My hovering spirit even recalls bits of conversation as Egor and I were preparing the potion.

"Do we just dump this stuff in the water or what?"

"No, Gregor, we must use an exact amount of rotenone for the exact amount of water in our study area. Why do you think we made a grid and took depth measurements?"

"I don't know. I'm just in this for the fish, not the math."

"We must be extremely careful when we mix the powder with the water in the barrel. We wouldn't want to contaminate our control area with an excess of our agent, would we?"

"How much of this stuff are we supposed to use, anyway?"

"One part rotenone to one hundred parts water."

"That doesn't sound like much. Where'd you get those numbers?"

"Oh, believe me, Gregor, it's plenty; the instructions are right up there in the pickup."

"Want me to get 'em to make sure?"

"Oh no, no, I've been over them many times. You just sit tight."

Thus the morning passed with Egor steering and sitting by the hose from the drum in the back of the boat, making sure the rotenone passed directly through the motor's propeller for even distribution, while I sat in the bow, dabbling my hand in the water. Soon a few fish started to twitch to the surface in our designated area. Then many fish started to twitch to the surface in our designated area. Then many, many fish started to twitch to the surface far beyond our designated area. Then the whole arm of the lake was so atremble with dying fish that Egor, at last, felt compelled to walk to the pickup and double-check the instructions.

"What's it say, Egor?"

"It says *mumble*, parts per *mumble*."

"What's that? I can't hear you."

"It says one part per thousand."

"I guess that sort of blows the whole deal, eh?"

"I guess."

So after reporting in to Dr. Frankenstein and observing the way his fury led him to the brink of tears, we returned to the lake every day for a week and cleaned up all of the dead fish with dip nets. On the second day, we netted just a few fish from the surface, and our hopes rose that the mayhem might not be too widespread. On the third day, our hearts began to sink as many more bobbed to the surface, and a familiar smell began to fill the air. On the seventh day we poled our boat for hours in the summer heat, gagging and straining the foul putrescence of the surface with our dip nets for corpses so decomposed that many dripped through the mesh, leaving only the gelatinous heads and spines.

The second of these tales from the crypt is shorter but no less horrifying. Lothar, another of Dr. Frankenstein's protégés, was in charge of several small holding ponds behind the dam on Lake Carl Blackwell, and in each of these ponds were over a thousand channel catfish. This was in the early days of catfish farming, and the ponds were part of a project to ascertain how fat a fish became from eating a controlled amount of food in a controlled space over a controlled period of time. I, Gregor, was particularly enamored of this project because of the "controlled" part. I had participated in a less controlled project on a larger pond near Stillwater where researchers kept catfish in huge cages that were strung on a cable.

It was my job as stoop labor to put a length of iron rebar through a loop at one end of the cable and rotate it end over end, thus tightening said cable and raising the cages from the water so that a graduate student might check the general condition of the fish. Once, when my partner said, "Wow, look at the size of this one," I released the iron bar to have a better look, the cable loosened, the cages went splooshing back into the water, and the rebar mumblety-pegged my foot.

But these ponds were different: no iron bar, no cable, no cages—just a feeding bin on a dock at one end and an adjustable spillway at the other. Life was good, especially at feeding time, when I would open a little hatch on the bin, release some pellets and watch the tumult of fat, healthy, dumb catfish fighting for their share while, at the other end, Lothar would adjust the water level to accommodate the condition of the experiment's ever-growing subjects.

Then one evening after a routine round of feeding and adjusting, the spillway only appeared to be well adjusted. Actually, it was very poorly adjusted. One might even say it was pathological. The next morning when Dr. Frankenstein drove out to observe the progress of his pet project, all the water was gone from that pond, and all the fish were dead. Because there was no water, I, Gregor, couldn't use a dip net as a distancing device. A shovel is a much more intimate tool, especially on the seventh day.

Though I had assisted Egor and Lothar in failing Dr. Frankenstein, there was still Renfield—Renfield the light of heart, Renfield the sound of mind, Renfield the deft of method, Renfield the lord of telemeters. Renfield's project involved following flathead catfish around. It never became clear to me, Gregor, why he followed them, but he certainly had the most advanced of telemetric technology to aid him in his pursuit, and that was fine by me.

Flathead catfish were just a notch below carp on my totem pole of deities. Years before, I had watched Cliff, the owner of Cliff's Restaurant in Stillwater, come bumping up against the dock near the boat ramp at Lake Carl Blackwell, the bottom of his boat filled with panting flathead catfish. When I say "filled," I don't mean a lot of catfish. I only mean one or two. They were huge.

Thus when Dr. Frankenstein gave me orders to accompany Renfield on his mission, I was more than gung ho. I'm not sure how Renfield came by his beluga flatheads, though I think he hung around the docks when guys like Cliff pulled up with their panting cargo and paid them good money. I clearly remember two large round cattle tanks with blurbling aerators

in a heated shed near the lake. I also remember massive dark
shapes moving around the bottoms of those tanks.

One morning, Renfield and I wrestled a fish from one of
the tanks into a large net and dealt with it in true Frankenstein
style. First we put the monster in a tub of anesthetic to calm
it down, then we hoisted it out and plopped it on an operat-
ing table, where Renfield deftly made an incision in its abdomen and planted something that went *click, click* in it so that
it began to writhe.

"Do not fret, My Pretty," said Renfield. "Soon you will be
well; soon you will be free."

"What's the *click, click* thing?" said I, Gregor.

"It's a telemeter."

"What's a telemeter?"

"It's a tracking device. With this technology, we shall be able
to follow My Pretty to the ends of her universe."

Then Renfield stitched up His Pretty and put her in the
other cattle tank, which was laced with a mild solution of anti-
biotics, and she rested until we released her into Lake Carl
Blackwell two weeks later. We followed Renfield's Pretty and
three of her colleagues around for about a week, but then we
lost track of them. I piloted our boat for several frantic days
while Renfield leaned woefully off the bow, his little box with
its antenna at the ready, but he couldn't detect a single click.

Finally, one gloomy day, I steered our boat into a dismal
little lagoon, and Renfield bolted upright in the bow.

"I'm getting clicks; I'm getting clicks. Go straight, no, left,
no, right—yes, that's it. My Pretty, we have found you."

"What's that?" I said.

"It looks like a big piece of Styrofoam. She must be under it."

But she wasn't under it. She *was* it.

Hurty, Hurty

I wonder how many erstwhile biologists are out there whose endorphins go ape shit when they can find little living things, chase them down, grab them and have a good look at them; yet when numbers rear their ugly equations in statistics, organic chemistry, quantitative analysis, and so on, their minds shut down like a dormant sea monkey. Mine sure did.

I chugged right along into my junior year in college, happily memorizing phylum, class, genus and species of whatever showed up in my dissecting tray or out in the field. But then two things brought me up short. One of the things, as I've already mentioned, was numbers; the other thing was Dr. Daphnia, my advisor. I called him that because he seemed to bounce around the classroom and the life sciences building like a huge water flea. He was also an invertebrate zoologist.

I referred to him by his profession once to Father, who was then the head of the English Department, and he chuckled, as if I'd made a little joke.

"That's a good one, son, an invertebrate zoologist."

"But that's what he is."

"Damned straight, *chuckle, chuckle*. I've met a few invertebrates myself, though they are usually in the humanities."

I didn't think Dr. Daphnia was spineless; I just didn't appreciate his teaching and advising methods. In the classroom he would try to spice up his lectures by making lurid comparisons between echinoderms, tornaria larvae and the canned eroticism of the latest James Bond movie. More than his lectures,

I remember the bookish young woman at the desk in front of me drawing clams and starfish with huge penises protruding from them.

His advising went something like this: "So, what are your interests? How shall we direct your major?"

"Well, I really like fish."

"Son, I'm afraid that's just not going to cut it."

"Can't I major in some kind of fish thing? Marine biology or limnology or fish and wildlife?"

"I suppose eventually you might focus your career in one of those directions, but you need a more credible reference, say, natural history." Soon I found out that Dr. Daphnia's hobby was natural history and he just wanted to entertain himself by having me specialize in it.

I did, however, appreciate Dr. Daphnia's humanity. Sometimes, I would help him in his lab, where he wore a little white jacket and fumbled around with beakers, test tubes and Bunsen burners. Cookie, a young woman who had attended my high school a year or two ahead of me, also worked in the lab. She wore a little white lab coat too, and it sometimes appeared to be all that she wore because the skirt under it was so short.

When she was around, Dr. Daphnia would experience considerable difficulty in conducting his research. Once when she was standing on a stool, stretching to get a bottle of acetone from a top shelf, Dr. Daphnia lost his concentration and lifted a boiling beaker from a Bunsen burner with his bare hand. Because he considered himself a gentleman, he said nothing but, "Hurty, hurty," then made sort of an *oomp, oomp* noise, hunched over, went into another room and closed the door. Through the door, Cookie and I could hear a muffled "Sweet Christ, fuck me running." Then Dr. Daphnia reappeared as if nothing had happened.

Lee Harvey Keeler

The same summer Cookie and I were learning to appreciate Dr. Daphnia's humanity, I also worked at the Oklahoma State Cooperative Fisheries Unit when it was in its pre–Dr. Frankenstein stage. I can't remember the last name of the professor who headed it up then, but his first name was Brad. Because I admired him and because his protégés never unleashed the horrors of science upon the local fish population, I'll go with his real first name and refer to him henceforth as Dr. Brad.

For want of a better term, I admired Dr. Brad for his ballsiness. He was a New England Yankee with connections to the mythic Woods Hole Oceanographic Institute, but more than that, he was a raging civil rights advocate. On his office wall hung pictures of Martin Luther King Jr. and Medgar Evers. Shortly after Dr. Brad arrived, I was riding in the front seat of a vehicle between him and a graduate student who hadn't yet seen the pictures on his wall.

"What's the difference between a black crappie and a white crappie?" said the graduate student.

"Don't you think that's rather obvious?" said Dr. Brad, taking his eyes momentarily off the road.

The graduate student winked at me and Dr. Brad. "No, I mean a BLACK crappie and a WHITE crappie."

I sank down in the seat as an almost tangible steam started to rise from Dr. Brad. "All right," he said, "let's hear it. What's the difference?"

"OK," said the graduate student, snorting in anticipation of his own punch line, "a BLACK crappie hangs out with carp and pushes worms to juvenile white crappie, and a WHITE crappie . . ." but he never got to the rest of the punch line because Dr. Brad had skidded to a stop, gotten out of the pickup, walked around to the passenger side, opened the door and firmly grasped the graduate student's arm.

"What's the difference between a bigmouth racist and a smallmouth racist?" said Dr. Brad. I don't remember what happened after that, except no one got hurt and the graduate student was a little more discriminating in his topics of conversation when he was around Dr. Brad.

I recount this story because, for a much different reason, I also experienced the wrath of Dr. Brad. Owing to the influence of Dr. Daphnia and the stone wall that mathematics had thrust up before me, I had decided to become an English major. Not only did I figure that English might be more accommodating to my right brain, I had also watched my father *be* an English professor for years and thought I had a better idea of what I was in for. I had told none of this to Dr. Brad but had rationalized that it would be best for him to find out at some point in the nebulous future, when I was at a relatively safe distance from his office. I knew that, because of my politics and my fascination with fish, Dr. Brad liked me and was looking forward to mentoring me into the profession. I didn't know that the graduate student who had told the crappie joke had discovered my curriculum change and had dutifully informed Dr. Brad.

Thus, one August afternoon in the summer of 1967 when I was sitting in a small room slicing cross-sections from catfish spines with a little circular jewelry saw and mounting them on slides for an age/growth project, Dr. Brad appeared at the door.

"What are you majoring in, Greg?"

"Uh, I've been majoring in zoology." I thought that perhaps

the present perfect might cloak the truth of my situation, but Dr. Brad would have none of it.

"I didn't ask you what you HAVE BEEN majoring in. I asked you what you ARE majoring in."

Then I decided to be upfront and manly, to hit him with the cold, hard truth. After all, who was he to question my plans for a career in literature?

"I'm sorry, sir. I was going to tell you, sir. It's the gosh-darned math, sir. I just couldn't cut it, sir. I really, really like you, sir, and I really, really don't want to let you down. I just figured that maybe I could approach fisheries management better from a, well, a literary perspective, sir."

"So, you're an English major. Maybe you didn't WANT to let me down, but you HAVE let me down," he said, and he did look genuinely hurt. "Don't expect to have a job here next summer."

After he left, I didn't just feel that I had let him down. I felt that somehow I also had failed the Kings, the Everses and the Kennedies. Byron De La Keeler, Lee Harvey Keeler. And I didn't have a job there until a year later, when Dr. Brad went on to greener, more liberal pastures, and Dr. Frankenstein replaced him.

Kept Fish

. . . .

I have spent much of my life keeping fish in aquariums. The fascination started when my brother brought one home with some tropical fish when we lived in Virgil, New York. Names like zebra danio, gourami, black molly, swordtail and angelfish were enough to get my blood pumping, but the sight of neon tetras under an aquarium light were too much for my young psyche to bear. I'd watch them for hours, not knowing what else to do. I started keeping my own fish in Stillwater when I was eleven and persisted in keeping them intermittently for the next thirty-four years.

I finally stopped after visiting David Duncan, my friend who wrote the fishing novel *The River Why*. When I saw his Ahab-drowning bass, I realized that any attempt I might make at harboring fish might easily be construed as boring and redundant.

There in his backyard in Portland, David had two small concrete fishponds that he had illegally stocked with small bluegill and bass. This in itself was enough to set my heart racing, but he hadn't just put them there; he had also trained them to eat a small orange lure fished on the end of a four-inch-long pliable plastic fishin' pole by a Lego man who rode around the pond in a six-inch-long yellow plastic life raft. When the fish would take the hookless lure, they would pull the Lego fisherman out of his raft and tow him around underwater for an amazingly long time, plenty long enough to drown him as thoroughly as Moby Dick did Ahab.

But in retrospect, I think the Ahab-drowning bass was only part of my reasoning when I returned my last kept fish to the pet store. Perhaps because I was getting older and more world-weary, I started identifying more with my fish. After all, they have eyes, noses and mouths (what Lynda Sexson, another friend, once called "faces"), and seeing them confined to such strict quarters in such a tiny chunk of their element started to remind me of, well, me. Every time I looked into their eyes, I couldn't help but project my own circumstances.

With that projection in mind, I present you with the following one-act psychodramas, each based upon various fish I've kept in various aquariums over the years.

A Fish Tank Named Desire

Cast of Characters:
Huck: A juvenile longear sunfish caught from Lake Carl
    Blackwell
Blanche: A slightly larger bluegill sunfish caught from
    Stillwater Creek
Jim: A small carp (but larger than Blanche) caught from
    Stillwater Creek
He: A boy

Setting:
A fish tank in the living room of Greg (to whom the fish refer as "He") and his family. A ceramic diver stands at one end and a large red rock at the other. The tank itself resembles one of those glass bricks one sees surrounding the entrances of Chinese restaurants built in the forties and fifties, except for its open top and its unusual dimensions: 24 inches by 24 inches by 6 inches. The year is 1958.

Blanche: Stay away from my rock.
Huck: Sorry, I don't know why, but I have this strange compulsion to . . .

Blanche: Whatever it is, do it to the diver.

Huck (straining and fanning his tail over the diver's head): Who's your daddy?

Blanche: Christ, get a room. Hey look, it's Him, and He's coming over here!

Both (bumping their noses against the front of the tank): Food, food, food!

Blanche: What the hell?

Greg upends a coffee can and releases Jim into tank.

Huck: Ahhhhhhhhh!!

Blanche: Ahhhhhhhhh!!

Jim: Ahhhhhhhhh!!

All dart madly around the tank for a few seconds and then settle down with Blanche on one side of the rock, Jim on the other and Huck behind the diver.

Huck: I want my mother.

Jim: You appear to be about that age, but believe me, it makes for some screwed-up kids. *(turning toward Blanche)* Haven't we met somewhere before?

Blanche: You're from Stillwater Creek, right?

Jim: First pool below the Western Street Bridge. Who's the perch?

Huck: I'm not a perch.

Blanche (ignoring him): He thinks he's a whale, but he doesn't know his Moby from his Dick.

Huck: What's a dick?

Suddenly Greg's face looms large before them, and he plinks the side of the tank with his fingernail.

All: Food, food, food!

The End

The Elephant Boy

Cast of Characters:
Camille: An adult bluegill
Marilou: An adult green sunfish
Dean: An adolescent crappie
Greg: An adolescent boy (to whom the other characters
　　refer as God)

Setting:
A standard-sized aquarium in Greg's room. There is a fishnet partition down the middle. Camille and Marilou are
on one side of the partition, and Dean is on the other. The
year is 1962.

*Greg drops a few little bread balls in with Camille and Marilou,
and they eat them halfheartedly.*
Camille: I can't believe we were dumb enough to let Him catch
　　us on these things. They taste like leftover shit.
Marilou: That's redundant.
Camille: Whatever.
Marilou (to Dean): Hey, ASSHOLE.
Dean (obsessed with his reflection on glass, ignores her): Lookin'
　　kinda good.
Marilou: Gag.
Camille (to Marilou): My fins seem to be healing up pretty well.
　　How 'bout yours?
Marilou: I'm still missing a sizable piece of tail. (*To Dean*)
　　Thanks, ASSHOLE.
Dean (to reflection): What YOU lookin' at? Yeah, YOU. What
　　you LOOKIN' at?
Camille: I think I'm gonna puke.
Marilou (looking at Greg): Praise be to God that He put in the

partition, or no telling what ASSHOLE would have done to our tails.

Greg opens the closet, takes a stuffed elephant from the shelf and then sits on bed.

Marilou: Isn't He a little old for that?

Camille: Who, him?

Marilou: No, Him. Good God! What's He doing to the elephant!

Camille: Who, him?

Marilou: No, Him.

Finis

Macbass

Cast of Characters:
Macbass: A four-pound largemouth bass
Greg: A young English professor
Judy: Greg's wife

Setting:
A standard-sized aquarium on Greg and Judy's back patio in Natchitoches, Louisiana. Greg has put Macbass in the aquarium, which is only a few inches longer than Macbass, so that he might ponder Macbass's mysteries for a little while before he cleans him. The year is 1974.

Macbass: Get on with it.

Greg: What you thinking, big fella?

Macbass: Get on with it.

Judy: What are you doing out there?

Greg: Just having a little talk with Mr. Bass here.

Macbass: Get the bloody hell on with it.

Judy: I don't think Mr. Bass can participate in the conversation.

Greg: Au contraire, Mr. Bass's expression says it all.

Macbass: Read my lips. Get (*buh buh*) on (*buh buh*) with (*buh buh*) it (*buh buh*).

Lights dim.

As the Whirl Turns

Cast of Characters:

Laura: A young angelfish

Leland: An old, fatherly, fantail goldfish

Bob: A large, dark, tropical catfish who lives behind a big rock and blends in with the gravel bottom during the day and zooms around the aquarium during the night

Gregory: A depressed middle-aged man

Judith: Gregory's wife

Setting:

A large aquarium in the living room window of Gregory and Judith's home in Bozeman, Montana. The year is 1994.

Laura: Like, Leland, like, wake up!

Leland: Wha, who, where? Oh, whew, it's you. Thank God you're alive. I dreamed that He had you (*points nose at Gregory, who is glumly pacing in a circle beside the aquarium*). But it wasn't really Him. It was actually him (*points nose at Bob's rock*). I don't want to think about what he was going to do to you.

Laura: Like, look at yourself in the glass. You're like—white with tiny black dots!

Leland: Noooo! That was part of the dream too! I went from golden boy to geezer overnight.

Bob suddenly zips out from behind his rock and starts zooming in a tight circle around the bottom of the tank.

Laura: Like, help!

Leland: Get behind me. He'll have to come through me before he gets my angel.

Laura: I feel, like, weird.

Leland: It's okay; he's behind his rock again.

Laura starts panting and whirling in circles.

Leland: Stop that, Angel, you're making me dizzy.

Laura: I, like, can't help it. It feels like I'm, like, caught in something.

Leland: Look, He's bringing the dip net. He's going to make you well.

Gregory (dips up Laura and looks at her in net): Poor little angel-fish. Looks like the whirling disease is infecting all of us.

(leaves room with Laura in net)

Leland: Hey, where are you going with my angel? Come back!

Sound of toilet flushing

Leland: Nooooooo.

Lights dim, then come up again on Bob resting comfortably at the bottom of an otherwise empty aquarium. Gregory has left Judith, and now she is walking glumly in circles beside the aquarium.

Judith: Darkness surrounds us.

Bob: And?

Part II

He hung a grunting weight.

Elizabeth Bishop, "The Fish"

Sex, Freud
and Fishing Poles

. . . .

It is the spring of 1968, and Greg is now a senior in college. He and his fiancé, Edith, are lying naked on a blanket beside the Cimarron River. Though he has had several girlfriends, he has "saved himself" and continues to do so, perhaps to the chagrin of Edith. She has recently given him an Easter card with a bunny on the front. Inside, the card says, "All this bunny wants in her Easter basket is you." He was so taken with the card that he showed it to his mother and father, with whom he is still living while he finishes college. His mother and father are both followers of the psychologist Sigmund Freud, so his mother says, "Aha, I guess we know what THAT means," and his father winks knowingly.

And perhaps, for the time being, Edith does want Greg in her Easter basket, but all that is about to change, for while the two of them are lying naked on the blanket in one another's arms, he is occasionally glancing up at a fishing rod that he has propped on a sandstone rock by the river and baited with a worm he has dug from the bank with his hands. He had mistaken the look of stunned amazement on Edith's face while he dug the worms, put them on his hook and set his rod for the look of pride and satisfaction that he has seen on his mother's face when she has watched him perform these tasks. His father has brought him to this place to fish for many years, here where the Cimarron winds under Ripley's Bluffs, where profuse redbud blossoms nod over their reflections on the eddies and backwaters and bass and sunfish inhabit the sandstone pools in the adjacent cedars.

Look, look, Greg has a bite. Oh, what will he do? Will he ignore this remnant of his simple, gender-neutral youth and direct his full attention to this bunny and her basket, or will he tear himself from her arms and rush to the riverbank?

It appears that he hasn't even realized there is a choice involved here.

"I'll be right back," says Greg.

Not Exactly an Abba
Dabba Honeymoon

. . . .

Dear Mom,
The fishing is great. The flight from Oklahoma City to
Brownsville was great. George Nigh, the Lieutenant Gover-
nor, was on our plane on the trip down and wished us well.
Port Isabel is great. Padre Island is great.
　Love,
　Greg

Thus during the first day of the honeymoon, we find Greg
standing in the surf before a hotel. Is he frolicking with his
beloved? Can we allude to Burt Lancaster and Deborah Kerr
awash in sea foam on the beach in *From Here to Eternity*? But
what is this we see in his hand? Surely it's not the gleam of
chrome on his Zebco spin-casting reel? Surely he's not catching
whiting on chunks of shrimp and cooking them that evening
on a grill and charcoal provided by the hotel?

That night as we peer into their beachfront hotel room that
looks out over the white line of the moonlit surf, are we to witness the torrid passions of a long-awaited consummation? Not
so much. This bunny has firmly realized that she doesn't want
this fishing mechanism in her basket. See the fishing mechanism trudge down the stairs to the beach. See it plod restlessly

And what is Edith thinking, sunbathing there on her towel,
then later in her deck chair, watching his face, illuminated
over the grill?

up and down the surf, first wondering how love went wrong, then wondering if anything might be biting out in those moon-lit breakers.

The next day, who is this, lying seasick on a bench in the hold of a pitching charter boat? Could it be our beautiful young bride? She is so sick, she can't even wonder, "What have I done?" Up on the deck, her groom is having a whee of a time. He is standing between two nurses from a Houston hospital, and they are catching grouper and snapper as quickly as they can retrieve them—and that is pretty quickly because the skipper has provided them with electric reels. Now her groom has just caught a huge red snapper. Its tongue is swollen and its eyes are bugging out because it has been pulled from the depths so quickly that the skipper had to throw water on the smoking electric reel. Now her groom, in all of his genius, is descending the steps into the hold to show her his trophy.

Somewhere there is a picture of the giant snapper on a banquet table surrounded by Greg's parents and their friends. Greg has left it with them; then, with his new bride, he has flown to California and Peace Corps training.

A Rowboat on
the Bosporus

Now it is a year later, and Greg is rowing a boat on the Bosporus near Istanbul. He isn't sure where Edith is. Even though he chose to momentarily abandon her for a twitching fishing rod, she decided to marry him anyway. After all, the bridesmaids had bought their dresses, and the honeymoon had been planned. At the wedding ceremony, Greg said what the minister told him to say. He was puzzled that Edith spoke gibberish when it was her turn to say things, but the minister didn't seem to mind, so neither did Greg. Somewhere, there is a picture of Edith feeding him a piece of the wedding cake. In the picture, Edith's face looks like it is exploring another galaxy though her hand is there above his mouth.

They are in Turkey because neither of them wanted Greg to go to Vietnam, so they enlisted in the Peace Corps. Their first choice was Colombia, their second choice was anywhere in South America, and their third choice was anywhere in the Western Hemisphere; but because there were so many young men who had decided that the Peace Corps might be a better option than Vietnam, they had to settle for Turkey.

For newlyweds whose relationship is already doomed, it has been an unfortunate assignment because, as the young couple has learned in cross-cultural training, the illusions cast by the American movie industry have caused many Turkish men to think that American women are prostitutes. Thus, after spending her days trying to teach English but instead being treated like a whore, Edith must return to her home and her bed with Greg.

So here in Istanbul, Edith has suggested that, for the day, he find something to do without her, and she, in turn, will find something to do without him. He almost started to wonder what Edith was doing without him when he saw some brightly colored rowboats bobbing out on the Bosporus. In these boats were Turkish men with hand lines. Then, with the sun flashing on the waves in the foreground and the minarets of the great mosque, Aya Sophia, towering in the background, Greg saw the gleam of a large fish as one of the men pulled it, hand over hand, into his boat.

With this image in mind, Greg overcame his fears and approached a young man in a café by the water and asked him if he might know how to rent a rowboat. It took some courage for him to overcome these fears because of his previous experiences in Turkey. For example, when he was on his way to his Peace Corps job teaching English at Ataturk University in Erzurum, Turkey, children would follow him to the bus stop shouting "Amerikan donkey" and throwing stones at him. In his literature class, he tried to make his students read Frank Norris's *The Octopus* because it was one of the only two novels available, but when he heard that one of his students, Zeki, was planning to shoot him, Greg told them that they could read the other novel, Ernest Hemingway's *The Old Man and the Sea*, instead. After they discussed the part where the sharks attack Santiago's giant marlin, Zeki said, "You are very tall, Mr. Keeler. Would you join me and my friends on the university basketball team?" "I'm sorry," said Greg. "I am very clumsy and do not play well." "It is OK that you do not play well because you are tall, and that is the thing that matters," said Zeki.

Soon Greg was in a large gymnasium crowded with Turkish men. He was ready to play poorly, but there was no place where he could change his clothes. "This does not matter," said Zeki. "These men will not mind if you change into your uniform here in the bleachers." Many of the men watched him as he changed into his uniform, but they didn't seem to mind. Greg played basketball even more poorly than usual because players on the other team would hit him in the head with their elbows and trip him when he tried to dribble the ball, but the referees didn't seem to mind. When he was finally allowed to go to the free throw line, he felt something wet on his arm as he started to shoot; he was surprised when he looked toward the stands because he hadn't realized that people could spit that far. After Greg lost the game for his team, Zeki approached him while he was changing back into his clothes in the bleachers and said that another teammate, Yusuf, wanted to fuck him, and would he mind? "Yes," said Greg. "Yes, I would mind."

He didn't know that some young Turkish men were driven by the strictures of their Moslem upbringing to fuck each other before marriage because Moslem women were so closely guarded by their families. Thus when Zeki told him that Yusuf wanted to fuck him, Greg rushed home, red-faced, to his young wife who would, most likely, have preferred that Greg stay there and let Yusuf fuck him.

But this young Turkish man in the café is fortunately in the process of courting an Englishwoman and has seized the opportunity to have an American translate a love letter for him, so with the aplomb of a seasoned guide, he bargained with one of the fishermen, and voilà, he and Greg are in this boat. They have fished with their hand lines for several hours but have not had a bite, so Greg is rowing and translating while Mustafa writes.

"OK, Greg, would I write, 'I am loving you for always'?"

"I think it would be better if you wrote, 'I will love you forever.'"

"Is 'forever' one word?"

"I don't know," says Greg. "I think so."

"For the next line, I will write, 'My arms are wanting to hold you,' OK?"

"She will like you more if you write, 'I long to hold you in my arms.'"

"I do not understand the way you are using the word 'long.'"

"It means you have been wanting to hold her for a long time."

"This is good. It is making sense. She will like this. Why are you crying?"

Black Sea
Perch Détente

. . . .

But hey, tears are a part of us all, right? And where is Gregory now? It is a month before the Bosporus, and he is on the Black Sea in Trabzon, Turkey, standing on one of the many boulders that line the harbor. He is holding a spinning rod and casting out into the mist and slate-gray waves. Around him are three or four airmen approximately his own age from the Air Force base directly behind them. Every time he casts, one of the airmen shouts, "Hair of the dog," or "I'll drink to that." Greg is thinking of the day before and of Erkut, a Turkish man who drove him and Edith from the university where they work in Erzurum over winding mountain roads through lush, fogged valleys and villages down to this small city by the sea. The airmen call Erkut "Tom" because he grew up in his father's shop, helping him to tailor suits for NATO flyboys, as he calls them, and he speaks perfect vernacular English.

Tom understood that there was something sad between the young couple beside him. He didn't have to understand that there was something sad between the father and young boy in the backseat, for he was driving them to a surgeon in Trabzon who might be able to repair the boy's cleft palate, which caused a wet, sucking noise each time the child took a breath. Tom did his best to improve the mood in the vehicle.

"So Greg, what are you and Edie planning to do in Trabzon?"

"Eat pork; we haven't had any since we came to Turkey."

"Oh, I see, you'll eat that for your Easter holiday tomorrow, right?"

"Right."

Except for the child's breathing, the silence continued for a few miles until Edith said, "How do they do it?"

"Who?" said Tom.

Edith pointed to a group of colorfully dressed women walking up the steep road through the fog carrying huge bundles of sticks on their heads. "Them. They seem so small to carry so much. Look, they're even laughing."

Tom rolled his window down and shouted something in Turkish, and they shouted back, then continued laughing.

"What did you say?" said Edith.

"I told them that they work too hard."

"And what did they say?"

"They said it beats freezing."

"They're beautiful," said Edith.

"I know," said Tom.

Now Greg's thoughts are interrupted, and he's brought back to the present because he has a bite.

"I've got one—a nice one," says Greg.

"I'll drink to that," says the airman.

Out in the harbor, some Russian sailors watch from their ship as Greg drags a large ocean perch flopping to the rock beside him. Because the only English they know is from American movies, one shouts, "Go for your gun, Johnny," and slaps his hip, and the airman shouts, "I'll drink to that." In his mind, Greg is comparing the perch on the rock beside him to a document on a table at a superpower summit. He wants to share this with Edith, but she is somewhere else.

The Acrep
Has Bitten

* *

And now he is on another sea and another season. The sea is
the Mediterranean, and the season is summer. But wait, he
is not fishing; he, in fact, appears to resemble a beached fish
himself, on his knees here in this isolated cove, mouthing *why,
why* into the breakers. Edith, the night before, told him that
she has gone elsewhere for the love she couldn't find with him.
Some might be astounded that Greg would feel compelled to
pose this question to the breakers, since the answer would
seem so obvious.

Greg and Edith have been working at a summer camp for
underprivileged Turkish children from the nearby town of
Antalya. On the second day there, after they had helped to set
up the camp, he left Edith with the other volunteers, picked up
a hand line and charged down to the surf, where he fished for
so long that his back blistered and his calves turned into large
red footballs from sun poisoning. On a more recent night, he
had rowed out beyond the breakers in a dinghy with the Turkish cook and fished for hours by lantern light, only to catch
one odd fish that the cook held up, saying, "You eat, you die,"
before he threw it back. And then, on this most recent night,
the night that has brought Greg to his knees here in this cove,
he and Edith, at the suggestion of their friend Stu, the Peace
Corps physician, had each consumed a tin of a cough suppressant known as Romular.

Neither Greg nor Edith needed to suppress a cough. Because
it is the late sixties and because neither of them wanted to

suffer the consequences of obtaining illegal substances, they consumed this medication for its hallucinogenic effect. Greg very quickly wished that they had not followed their friend's suggestion, for, as he and Edith walked on a public pier in the Antalya harbor, he temporarily lost his vision and the use of his legs. The cough suppressant's effect had not been quite so complete for Edith, so, with the help of another Peace Corps volunteer, she guided Greg to an apartment, where they lay on a cot and Greg slowly regained his vision while Edith, deprived by the drug of her social filters, bared her heart to him.

"Greg, I screwed someone."

"Screwed?"

"Yes, screwed, I screwed someone."

"Who'd you screw?!"

"Stu, I screwed Stu."

"You screwed Stu?!"

"Yes, I screwed Stu."

And what will Greg do now that the breakers have not answered his question but have, instead, gone up his nose, and a jellyfish has drifted into his swimming trunks and stung him there? The simple and immediate answer is this: He will go fishing.

The more complicated and extended answer is this: He will try to pretend that nothing happened, but circumstances will not allow Greg to maintain this pretense. A few nights later, on his way from their tent to the latrine, Greg will step on a scorpion, and then he will shake it from his foot and step on it again. Edith will accompany Greg and Rodney, another Peace Corps volunteer who was simultaneously bitten, as a driver navigates the road along the steep cliffs to Antalya. There a doctor will give Greg and Rodney injections of horse serum; then they will go to a dilapidated villa, sit on its patio overlooking Antalya harbor, get drunk and scream obscenities at the stars until dawn. The morning they return to the camp, a scorpion will climb out of the bread bin and bite the Turkish cook's helper on the arm. The young helper will not be driven to town for a shot, and he will not get drunk and sit screaming at the stars all night. He will just say three words in English and one word in Turkish: "The acrep has bitten." He will then sit pensively by the sea all day and return to work that evening.

The next week, after Greg recovers from his bites, he will contract an especially virulent strain of influenza so that his temperature climbs to one hundred and four degrees and he is placed in a tin tub of ice and water so that it won't climb any higher. When he finally recovers, he will not look much like a counselor at a summer camp for Turkish children. Rather, he will resemble a resident of the Confederate prison camp at Andersonville—except for his lovely tan.

Besides the other Peace Corps volunteers, the Turkish cook and his helper, there are two high school students, Ted and David Scherrer, working at this summer camp. Their father is General Scherrer and he commands the U.S. Military Mission for Aid to Turkey. When he is flown down to visit his sons in his personal plane, he will see this tanned anachronism from Andersonville and come to know the circumstances that brought him to such a condition, and in his mercy and compassion, he will fly Ted, David, Edith and Greg back to Ankara, the capital of Turkey, and there he and his wife will treat the young couple as their own until they wish them a safe departure back to the United States.

Good Kids

. . . .

Less than a month later, here he is again, wading in his swimming suit, but this time he is fishing in the Delaware River and Edith is swimming beside him. They have recently returned from Turkey, and, while visiting Greg's brother in Cambridge, where he is attending MIT, they saw a poster advertising a concert called Woodstock and, at Edith's insistence, purchased tickets to the event. Because their minds were still unsettled from the restrictions of a Moslem society, they thought that it would be a pleasant way to ease themselves back into American culture.

Near Woodstock, cars were backed up for a mile, the gates had been torn down and thousands of people, the likes of whom Greg and Edith had never seen, were flowing down into a natural arena before a giant stage. On that stage was John Sebastian of the Lovin' Spoonful. He seemed to be at least as stunned by the situation as Greg and Edith, for all he could say was "like wow," and "like man" and "you're all, like beautiful." When they finally found a dry spot away from the mud, a voice besides John Sebastian's came echoing over the giant speakers, saying something like, "Take the green and white ones, but whatever you do, don't take the brown ones. They're like bad shit, man," and a young woman next to them, whose breasts were badly sunburned because she had removed her shirt, started screaming.

For the rest of the day, they listened to bands like Canned Heat, the Grateful Dead and the Incredible String Band while they tried to find a bathroom. That night, as a band played that someone near them called Mountain, Greg felt like he could identify with the lead singer, not because he was a rock star making huge frightening sounds but because, in the distance, the man himself was so tiny in contrast—the way he slumped to his little knees and contorted his little body before a tiny microphone.

But where were Greg and Edith going to sleep? There was no place even to lie down, except for a few unoccupied mud holes. So back to their little yellow VW bug convertible they trudged, through couples grunting and naked in the mud, through vast clouds of marijuana smoke, through the torn-down gates and down a mile of moonlit road. And that night they drove to town after town, staring hollow-eyed at No Vacancy signs until they finally pulled off to the side of a dirt road and slept in the car for the two hours before dawn.

The next morning brings us here to these little white cottages on the Delaware River, a mom-and-pop operation where both Mom and Pop expressed reservations when Greg and Edith pulled in this morning.

"May we have a cabin for two?" said Greg.

"Are you from that bunch of hippies up north?" said Pop.

"Oh no," lied Greg. "We've just returned from the Peace Corps."

"Yes," said Edith, "we were in Turkey."

"Oh my," said Mom. "You two have come a long way, and you do look tired. Let's give these kids the honeymoon cabin."

"Sure," said Pop, "I guess they're OK."

So for a short time, Greg and Edith came under the protection of this old couple. Pop offered Greg a rod and reel and his choice of lures, and Edith talked to Mom about Turkey and her home in Oklahoma.

Now, Mom and Pop are in their kitchen, fixing lunch for Greg and Edith while he fishes and she swims. But what is this coming down the road? A Volkswagen van? Headbands? Beards? India print dresses?

"Hey, man, is this like a beach?"

"No," says Greg, "We're just . . ."

"Yes," says Edith, happy to be in America, happy to see these young American men and these American women who would laugh if someone called them a whore. "It's a beach."

And here come Mom and Pop screaming, "Get off our property. We'll call the sheriff," and then, turning to Greg and Edith, "We thought you were good kids. Pack your things and get out. We don't want your kind around here."

The rest of their life together seems to accumulate speed and vanish to a dot behind Greg: the dismal time they spent in Oklahoma after they returned; Edith's departure for the freedom of San Francisco in 1970; the divorce and Greg's move to Idaho, where he and his Muskogee friend, Ken Cook, found a doctoral program that allowed them to fish and not write dissertations.

Greg and Edith have neither seen nor talked to each other in thirty-seven years. Greg sometimes wonders what might have happened if, on that late spring day on the Cimarron, he had not rushed to his fishing rod.

What's in a Name?

. . . .

See Greg. See Greg fish. It is the late summer of 1972, and he is in Idaho on Trail Creek about twelve miles northeast of Ketchum. But who is this sitting in his yellow VW bug convertible while he fishes? Could it be Muffet Hemingway? Surely not.

Greg has moved from Stillwater to Pocatello, Idaho, with his friends Ken and Ken's wife Vicki so that he might earn a doctorate of arts in English. Greg is enamored of this program because:

1. It is in the mountains.
2. It doesn't require a doctoral dissertation.
3. It offers him sufficient time to fish for trout.

Greg has also met a poet friend, Ricardo Sternberg, who helps him remain in his fantasy world of fishing so that he doesn't have to spend too much time thinking about things like the past and the future. For example, he and Ricardo caught a large rainbow trout, and while Ricardo's wife, Crissy, was slaving away as a waitress on the night shift at JB's Big Boy, they applied stripes of green, red and yellow food coloring while it was frying so that it would look like a rainbow trout, both before they cooked it and after.

Greg's life at this time, however, wasn't totally devoted to fishing and frivolity. He was also working part-time in the Idaho State University library stacks to help make ends meet. It was here in the spring, before the summer I mentioned at the beginning of this chapter, that he saw a tall young woman studying, and, despite his aforementioned ill-fated attempts at romance, he worked up his courage to approach her.

"Excuse me," said Greg. "What's your name?"

"That shouldn't be important," said the young woman.

"I'm sorry," he said, and he returned to taking books from his cart and putting them back in the stacks. He didn't know that the young woman wanted to meet him but didn't want him to have to deal with her name. A week later, she approached him as he was hanging newspapers on a rack and asked him to have coffee with her. Over coffee she said, "My name is Muffet."

"I'm Greg Keeler," said Greg. "Do you have a last name?"

"It's Hemingway."

"Oh."

"I didn't tell you that the other day because as soon as people hear the name, they start treating me like someone they think they already know."

"Oh," said Greg.

"I'm telling you that I'm Ernest Hemingway's granddaughter now because you seem different, and I think you liked me before you knew who I was."

"Thank you," said Greg, "I appreciate that," but inside his head, he was already cowering before the monolithic letters of a name that had loomed on his father's bookshelves when he was a child. Muffet's beauty, her ruddy complexion and strong white teeth, now shared her face with the man whose picture hung on the wall of his father's study, a man who knelt next to huge dead things, rifle or rod in hand, a man who cavorted with bulls in Pamplona, a man whose death had sent Greg's father into an extended depression.

"Would you like to go to Paris with me?" said Muffet. Greg's mind filled with ambivalence and caution because this was only the sixth sentence Muffet had ever spoken to him (not that he was counting). It would be an incredible act of reckless abandon if he were to co-opt himself to the whims of the beautiful, iconic creature before him. At twenty-six, hadn't he already subjected himself to enough romantic tragedy?

"Sure," said Greg.

But when he had managed to scrape together funds for such a trip and called Muffet to let her know that he was serious, no one answered—for two weeks. Greg didn't find this alarming. After all, she was Muffet Hemingway, and he was, well, Greg.

Two weeks later Greg received a letter that went something like this:

Dear Greg,
I decided to go to Berkeley instead of Paris. I hope you aren't angry. I have been given some business opportunities here and I can't pass them up. I would still like to see you. Can you come to Berkeley?
    Your Friend,
    Muffet

A week later, he was standing outside an upscale restaurant in Berkeley, trying to act like he had some business there. Through the slightly tinted glass, Muffet was leaning over a table talking to some earnest young man who wanted to use her name for something. Muffet had suggested that Greg might join them, but the young man had looked at him as if he were a parking lot attendant and had offered that he might be more comfortable "shagging" a burger and fries at an adjacent beer hall, but his stomach wasn't feeling very good, so he chose to stand outside the window trying to act like he had some business there.

The next day, he stood outside a large stone building on the Berkeley campus while Muffet had lunch with Margaret Mead. He was beginning to think that maybe he might have been better off, say, spending the summer clubbing rats in a sewer when Muffet emerged from the building and said, "OK, I'm finished. Do you want to go to the ballet?"

"Sure," said Greg, and within a couple of hours they were at the front door of a great hall where they were greeted by a formal gentleman who looked at Greg's frayed leather jacket and bell bottom trousers and said, "I'm afraid, sir, that we don't . . ." Then Muffet handed the man a little card, and he said, "Oh, I'm so, so sorry, sir. Right this way, Miss Hemingway."

After that, things started to pick up. During the day, Muffet would attend to her business commitments, and Greg would hang around his brother's apartment, where he was staying in Berkeley, or wander out on Berkeley Pier and catch crabs and odd-looking fish, and in the evenings, they would have dinner and then discuss poetry or go to a museum or attend an art exhibit.

One day, all of the best things about that summer came together for Greg, though it didn't seem that way at first. The morning started off well when he chartered a boat to fish for salmon out from the Golden Gate Bridge because the skipper, the bait boy and all of the clients were from Oklahoma. But then he realized that the other Oklahomans on the boat felt ill at ease because of the blond hair that trailed down to the middle of his back. While they were all proudly discussing their Oklahoma backgrounds, he said, "I'm from Oklahoma too."

"Oh yeah?" said the skipper. "What part?"

"Stillwater."

"Stillwater," said one of the clients, "that ain't Oklahoma."

"It sure ain't," said the bait boy.

"Hell," said another client, "that's more like being from Sausalito."

"Sausalito?" said Greg.

"Yeah, you know," said the bait boy, lisping the S's, "Sausalito —where all the fairies come from," and he pointed to a ferryboat chugging a few hundred yards off the bow.

Greg didn't know what to say then, but he didn't need to know because a twenty-pound salmon took his bait. The other Oklahomans were very quiet as he put it in the holding box.

When they arrived onshore, instead of putting the fish in one of the big plastic bags the skipper had provided, he carried the fish out where everyone on the dock could see it.

"I can tell what you're doin'," sneered one of the clients. "You're holdin' that fish out where everybody on the dock can see it."

"Yes," said Greg, "that's how fairies do things in Stillwater."

That afternoon, when Greg showed Muffet the salmon, she oohed and ahed and said stoic and profound things about it.

But his brother, Ted, who was trying to adjust to the pressures of being a young professor at Berkeley, soon tired of his presence in his apartment, especially after he stunk the place up by making a huge potato salad with eggs in it, so Greg kissed Muffet goodbye, and she promised to invite him to her father's house in Ketchum later that summer.

I Like to Walk

. . . .

On his way to Ketchum from Pocatello, Greg stopped in a field
of sage and rolled around in it. Not only did he feel like a big
happy dog, but also he wanted to smell like the Great Out of
Doors when he entered Jack Hemingway's house, even though
deep down he knew that no matter what he rolled in, he would
most likely smell like a Big Fool. It was still morning when he
arrived at the place on the Big Wood River. Muffet was up to
greet him, and Jack was in his bathrobe drinking coffee by the
kitchen counter.

"And what brings you to Ketchum?" said Jack, looking
directly into the eyes of the big, long-haired, sage-smelling
Fool-Thing that had entered his house.

Greg just wanted to point to Muffet, who was looking as
big and beautiful as ever that morning, and not say anything,
but instead he said, "I was hoping to take Muffet fishing up on
Trail Creek."

"That should be interesting," said Jack. "What kind of flies
are you planning to use?"

"Grasshoppers."

"It's a little late," said Jack, "but Joe's Hoppers should still be
working up there."

Then Greg decided to 'fess up because, in his haste, he had
not brought his fly rod. He had only brought his spinning rod
because he always carried it in the trunk of his car. "Actually,"
said Greg, "I mean real grasshoppers."

"Oh?" said Jack.

"Some hitchhikers broke the tip off my fly rod when they
slammed it in the trunk of my car," lied Greg.

"Oh," said Jack. "You should probably catch your grasshoppers down here before you go up near the pass. They might be few and far between up there."

In Greg's mind, Jack's tone of voice made him think of this exchange between a priest and a member of his parish:

"Actually, Father, I'm not going to put real money in the collection plate. I'm planning to use slugs."

"Ah, I see, my son. Well, you should probably find your slugs in the crawl space beneath the sacristy because they're few and far between up here."

On the way to Trail Creek, Muffet said, "My father likes to fish with flies."

"I know," said Greg. "I hear he's pretty good at it."

"Yes," said Muffet, "he's a purist. He's that way about many things. He's also a Nixon environmentalist."

"You're lucky to have such an idealistic father," said Greg.

"Yes," said Muffet, "I'm lucky and he's lucky."

"Lucky to have you as a daughter."

"No," said Muffet, "just plain lucky. Last week he won a Mercedes-Benz in a raffle for Realtors."

"It sounds like he's pretty successful all the way around."

"Yes," said Muffet, "and he doesn't put up with any funny business from me and my sisters. I had a little too much to drink the other night, and the next morning he sent me on a twelve-mile hike—with a lousy hangover."

"It sounds like he cares about you."

"Yes, he does."

When they arrived at Trail Creek, Greg's head was spinning because it was grappling with the myth that Muffet had warned him against when they first met. As he baited up with the grasshoppers that he had caught in a field below, he asked Muffet if she would like to fish first.

"No thank you," said Muffet. "You fish. I'll just walk around for a while."

"OK," said Greg. So he fished. And fished. After a while, he returned and saw Muffet sitting in the car.

And who is this sitting in Greg's yellow VW bug convertible while he fishes? Yes, it is Muffet Hemingway. She smiles and waves at him, and he waves back. Then Greg continues to fish. Oh, the big sage-smelling Fool-Thing continues to fish. There is a beautiful young woman who likes him and is waiting for him in his car, and he continues to fish. The big sage-smelling Fool-Thing doesn't recognize the pattern. It continues to fish.

When, finally, he returns again to his car, there is no Muffet in it, so he searches for her—up the stream, down the stream, out in the meadow, into the forest—but no Muffet. Now Greg starts to think of, well, her. Has he hurt her feelings? Does she actually care about him? In desperation, he slowly drives down the hill and back toward town, peering up the hills and down the valleys. And there she is in the road ahead. What will Greg say? What can Greg say, stopping in the middle of the road, getting out of the car, going to her, wanting to cry but knowing he can't do that?

"I'm so sorry."

"Don't be sorry. You like to fish, I like to walk."

"I'm so, so sorry."

"I really, really like to walk."

And maybe she really does like to walk, rationalizes Greg as they drive the remaining miles to Ketchum, for she is already making plans for the afternoon and the evening—a dip in the hot springs and then a dance at the town hall where Idaho's favorite band, Tar Water, is playing.

They are the only ones at the hot springs, a fenced-in area, much like a swimming pool except that the water is hot. Muffet swims back and forth like a graceful animal.

Because he is not much of a swimmer, Greg sits mustache-deep in front of a hot jet of water and makes burbling noises while his hair floats around him like the tentacles of a jellyfish.

Muffet pushes her long elegant body out of the pool and reclines at one end, glistening in the afternoon sun. Greg slops himself up onto the concrete, bashing his knee and swearing in the process. He smiles at Muffet, but she looks away.

That evening, Greg goes to the dance with Muffet and her sister Margaux. He is wearing lineman boots that lace up to his knees because they make him feel manly and secure.

"Why are you wearing those boots?" says Margaux. "It will be hard to dance in them."

Muffet answers for Greg. "They're strong boots. He needs them because he spends lots of time outside."

"I thought he was a graduate student," says Margaux.

Inside the hall, Tar Water is playing their trademark combination of rock and bluegrass, which requires the less accomplished dancers to expend a great deal of energy by trying to make a move to every beat. The more accomplished dancers know how to choose their beats and move languidly and gracefully. As Margaux and Muffet both dance with Greg, they employ the latter method, while he employs the former.

Soon, because of his huge boots, he has an asthma attack and hunches wheezing and panting on one of the benches beside the dance floor.

"He's already worn out," says Margaux to Muffet. "He looked like such a big, strong man."

Wheeze.

"Are you OK?" says Muffet.

Wheeze.

That night, he sleeps in a room in the Hemingways' basement and awakens among pictures of Papa: Papa skiing with Gary Cooper, Papa in a beret drinking wine from a goatskin, Papa with a huge dead animal, Papa with a huge dead fish. Greg goes upstairs, and Muffet is sitting alone in the kitchen.

She says good morning and then says she needs to rest some more and goes to her room. While he stands there wondering what to do, a young girl enters. She appears to be eleven or twelve years old and is tall and pretty for her age, with her dark eyebrows and her piercing dark eyes. She sits down by a board game in an adjoining room.

"Hello, I'm Mariel. What's your name?"

"Greg."

"My sister is resting, but you can play with me if you want to."

"Sure," he says.

After a while, Muffet enters and tells Greg that her parents were up late and her mother doesn't want him in the house and maybe he should leave now.

"Sure," he says, but he is talking to Mariel because Muffet has already returned to her room.

On his way out of town, Greg stops to get gas and sees Margaux, who asks him if he is leaving already, and he tells her yes and that he is going fishing.

When he arrives at his parents' new house in Stillwater, Oklahoma, where he will spend the rest of the summer, he writes Muffet a letter, but for the return address, he absentmindedly puts the street number of his parents' previous house where he grew up. He is depressed for a month when Muffet never responds, but then he returns to Idaho and meets Judy, who will become his wife.

It is months later, after Greg has become thoroughly involved with Judy, that the letter Muffet wrote back to him reaches his parents at their new address, and they send it on to him.

The letter is written inside a card with M. C. Escher's lithograph *Three Worlds* on the front. In the lithograph are the reflections of leafless trees, their leaves forming a plane that is the surface of a pond, and a large fish beneath the surface.

Dear Greg:
Today I am Marcel Proust reincarnated. I only wish I could begin my manuscript to you as he would have liked, but I must surreptitiously continue in my own manner.

Gee, thanks for your letter. It made me feel so good. I have been bedridden and sick for the last two weeks. Lack of any energy. I got up for some iced tea today, which was exercise enough, and went back to sleep and dreamt 10 dreams, which is heartening and better than the picture shows 'cause you can solve the world's problems in a dream.

Wish I could tell you how great the baseball, swimming, tennis, bike riding is, but Muffet had none of it. Even my handwriting is shaky.

I want very much to go back to France and dream about that occasionally. Perhaps in about a month you could come up and visit, if my mom approves by then and I feel better. This card is a Mau Escher. I am writing a surrealistic book of poems with illustrations. Maybe I'll publish it some day. I did get to Poki one day and couldn't find you so went to West Yellowstone and that is when I started feeling weird. Have a great time in Stillwater—write soon.

Love,
Muffet

Over the years, Greg will sometimes see news of Muffet in magazines. He will see that she has written a novel with Paul Bonnecarrere called *Rosebud* and that it will be produced as a movie by Otto Preminger. He will see a picture of her with her famous four-bean salad at a Sun Valley picnic in *People* magazine. He will see her in an Oldsmobile ad with her father on television, saying, "This is not my father's Oldsmobile." He will think of her walking alone down the road off Trail Creek Pass.

Part III

Let me not to the marriage of true minds
Admit impediment.

William Shakespeare

Frogs in
Wheelchairs

. . . .

"Did you see that cartoon where frogs are rolling themselves around in little wheelchairs . . . ?"

My ears perk up. This party for English graduate students at Idaho State University has been fairly unremarkable until now, but this black-haired, blue-eyed woman sitting on the back of a couch in a gray miniskirt with one leg wrapped around the other has struck a chord, for I have had firsthand experience with legless frogs, so I interrupt her.

"They're outside of a French restaurant." I don't stand a chance with this woman. I get down on my hands and knees, bound across the room like a dog, put a hand on each of her shoulders and start licking her face. She finds this amusing. Her name is Judy.

Within a week, Judy, Judy's five-year-old son, Christopher, and I are standing on Cherry Creek, a few miles outside Poca-tello. I have caught a small trout and am clonking it on the head with a small rock.

"What's he doing, Mom?" says Christopher.

"He's clonking it on the head over and over again with a pebble."

"I can see that, but why is he doing it?"

"Why are you doing it, Greg?" says Judy.

"We're going to eat it, and I don't want it to suffer."

"I'm not going to eat it," says Christopher.

"It's still alive," says Judy. "Perhaps it would suffer even less if you used a bigger rock."

"No, a bigger rock might damage its flesh."

"Jesus Christ," says Judy, but she doesn't say any more on the subject because, as she will later come to admit, she and her son are living on welfare, and she is rather desperate to find someone to help support them.

For a year or two more, Judy and Christopher will humor me by occasionally standing streamside with me while I ignore them and clonk fish on the head, but gradually they will ease themselves away from the bank, and Judy will establish a home to which I will always return, and she will bear another son who will also decide that fishing is not for him.

But who is this Judy, and how is it that she maintains such a strong connection to this chronic fisherman? After all, she will not ooh and ah when I bring fish home and plop them into their kitchen sink. She will instead roll her eyes and say, "Nice ones, Greg." When I come home skunked with no fish, she will sing "Empty Stringer," a sardonic rendition of Lena Horne's "Stormy Weather." She will even occasionally spike my orange juice or lemon chiffon pie with Dexedrine or mescaline so that I might puzzle over my propensity for such frequent fishing trips—or at least become a little more interesting. She will finally admit that she does not even like to eat the fish that I catch, and seeing my hangdog expression, she will say, "If only you could catch brownies or fudge or cheeseburgers."

Sometimes I'll think that Judy is a hard woman as I sit in my corner eating my plate of fish while she and Christopher dig into their macaroni and cheese, but then I'll remember that Judy's life has perhaps been a little different from the norm.

A Little Doll

The man's breath smelled like onions when he took Judy's head between his hands and said, "There's something in your eye." Judy looked around the room to find the door, but the man's huge, whiskery face was blocking her view.

"Janet," he said, "go get a Kleenex."

Earlier that afternoon, Judy had been walking home from her first-grade class when she met Janet, who taught her how to play jacks. Janet was a nice change from the boys on the stoops who yelled mean things at her. She was getting to know her part of Brooklyn very well because her mother was always too busy listening to the radio or reading to accompany her to school or to the store where she sent Judy to buy her cigarettes.

Once a bus driver didn't see Judy because she was so little, and he hit her head with his front bumper. If there hadn't been several people screaming from the curb, he probably would have driven right over her. As it was, he just knocked her out. Judy wasn't mad that the bus driver had hit her because she got so much attention when she woke up, and while she was unconscious, she was in a big colorful tent in the desert, and beautiful women with thin pieces of cloth on their faces were giving her a bath.

When Judy's mother wasn't too busy reading, smoking or listening to the radio, she would sometimes call Judy her little doll and curl her hair and teach her to sing songs. Then, when Judy's mother's friends would come over, she would tell Judy to sing for them. Judy was very happy when this happened because everyone would be looking at her and smiling. When she was finished singing, they would say things like, "She's another Shirley Temple," or "She's so quick for her age," or "She's such a perfect little doll." Judy's mother was happy at these times, too, but as soon as the people left, she would tell her doll that she should be seen and not heard, or would she please run an errand to the store or since it's such a nice day, why didn't she go outside and play?

Sometimes after school, Judy would see the other little girls meeting their fathers at the front gate and wish that she had a father too. When she asked her mother where her father was, her mother would say that she had divorced him because he drank a quart of beer every evening and his feet smelled bad. Judy had seen one of the boys on the stoop drinking a quart of beer, and she understood how mean that could make someone, so when she tried to imagine her father, she could only see him holding a quart of beer and yelling mean things at her from a stoop. She had never smelled stinky feet, so she didn't know what that would be like.

Janet was in the third grade, and she told Judy that she didn't have a mother but she had a father who didn't drink beer or have stinky feet. After they had played jacks for a while, Janet invited Judy home to meet her father.

Judy knew that there was nothing in her eye, and while Janet's father held her head and breathed into her face, she thought that maybe beer and stinky feet might not be so bad after all, so just as he turned to get the Kleenex, she pushed his hands away, ran out the door, ran down the stairs, then ran across the street and into a drugstore where she leaned against a man who was standing in a line.

"My," said the man, "aren't we a little doll. Where's our mother?"

A Mail-Order
Daughter

. . . .

Toward the end of Judy's sixth year, her mother became a mail-
order bride to a wheat farmer in western Kansas, taking Judy
from a city of seven million to a farm where there was nothing
for what seemed like seven million miles in any direction. Her
new father never spoke to her ("Tell her to pass the potatoes."
"Tell her to feed the chickens." "Tell her to pick the beans.")
until she was old enough to drive the tractor, and then he said,
"Drive the tractor." So she drove and drove and drove the tractor in the sun with no umbrella but just a jar of water in a wet
towel, until she was so brown that people were surprised when
they saw up close that it was George Hagerman's stepdaugh-
ter and not one of the Mexican hands. After her stepfather
dragged her favorite horse to death behind his truck, screaming, *You whoor, you whoor*, she went to see *The Wizard of Oz*,
and thought, *What else is new?* When she began to have her
period, her mother wouldn't buy her Kotexes but would make
her wrap herself in flour sacks. Once when she came home
from college, the second floor of their house had jackrabbit
carcasses hanging from the ceiling where the chickens could
peck at them, and another time her room was full of chinchillas
taking dust baths in their cages.

At the University of Kansas she met and married a young man
who lost his sanity while she watched, a man whose phobias
were so bad that when a tornado alert came over their television,
he would run to their basement and drink himself unconscious.
Soon they separated, and she took their little boy to Idaho

for her first teaching job where, eventually, I came bounding
across a room on my hands and knees to lick her face.

Wedding

I with my new job
and you with your son, Chris,
decide that matrimony
is a must, so we kiss
sin and the sixties goodbye and head
for Elko, Nevada, and a no questions,
no blood tests, quick-fix solution.
The casinos, whorehouse trailers,
Basque food joints and shopping malls
all say THIS IS THE PLACE
TO MAKE SACRED OUR LOVE,
and after we find the grand courthouse,
the Justice of the Peace does,
as blue-haired court clerks
weep and clasp their hands
and Chris stares dumb
at his mom and new dad.
With no wedding rings,
we use those from your ears
then follow the Justice
to a private room where
he tells us some jokes
and of duck hunting in Cuba
before it fell—when everyone drove
Continentals and 300 ducks
could be shot in one day.
We say, how much do we owe.
He says, whatever it's worth.
So from a fat roll of twenties,
you pull out a five and we go.

Sunfish

Yes, Judy marries this huge puppy, and in the summer of 1973 they move to a small college town in northwestern Louisiana for its first full-time job, and they live on a bayou with a boat tied up behind the house, and she watches it row out and back on the Cane, an oxbow of the Red River, after its classes at the university, bringing bass, crappie and sunfish into the house in the vain hope that she and Christopher will have suddenly developed a taste for fish.

And they meet new friends, a philosopher, Fraser, and his wife, Dian; and Judy admires Fraser for his ability to be as droll as she about fishing; and it admires Dian for her ability to get down on her hands and knees and bounce backward while barking like a Pomeranian. And it starts calling Judy the "Bunny" because she, at least upon occasion, wants it in her Easter basket. And The Bunny mildly objects on the grounds that the name is diminutive and sometimes puts her in the role of a stuffed animal. But because both it and The Bunny are well aware that she is nothing of the sort, she lets this pass.

And in the fall, it drives The Bunny to the Natchitoches hospital because her water has broken and there she bears a son, Maxwell Alfred Keeler.

Birthday: September 1974
Natchitoches, Louisiana
for Judy

When St. Denis found this place
the Red River ran through it.
Back 260 years, he probably waited

for the cool weather too.
Between us, the steamboats
up through the middle of town
stopped with slavery and a flood
that sent the river somewhere else,
leaving this oxbow, the Cane,
where I park by a boat ramp
and watch a black woman
lift a gleaming string of sunfish
and an old boy gun
his bass rig onto a trailer.

Since Max was born this morning
the wind's been different all day:
more sluggish, thick with
the fried chicken smell of cottonseed oil
from a mill on the outskirts.
When the contractions started,
we drove the morning fast
through this wonder soup,
even thicker with the cabbage smell
blowing in from distant paper mills.
It all stopped at the hospital
where the doctor took me aside,
showed me the x-ray of your pelvis
and said it would be a breech.
For what seemed hours
they had you somewhere else,
and I watched them wheel
a huge black woman
in and out of her own room screaming.
The doctor went out for a sandwich
while we practiced our Lamaze charade.
In your first few puffs,

a foot came out and water
sprayed the labor room
to send the nurses screaming,
wheeling you away,
pushing me out to the quiet hall.
I tried to read, but
a whistle like a distant train
brought me back. It was you
in the delivery room, a scream
so high yet so abrupt, a quick
birth and no doctor. The nurse
with the It's a Boy button
seemed as unreal as Max later,
through the glass: purple,
bulldog-faced, head scarred.

A soft hand on my shoulder
turned me to a small black man
in sweat-stained work clothes.
"My wife, suh, she need a ride.
We got no car. They try to
make her ride the ambulance,
but that cost money we ain't got."
Down the hall was the huge woman
in a wheelchair with the hot baby
and a scowling white nurse.
The man took the baby, and I tried
not to stumble carrying the woman
into the car. His tiny mother followed,
staring at me as if I were
from another planet.
In the rearview I saw the nurse
and heard crows and a distant caw:
"If anything happens, they'll sue."

But I thought of you, lying drained,
trying to make sense of the nurse's story.
We stopped for a rare traffic jam
on a bridge over the Cane.
Finally, at the other side,
we saw a half-mile stretch
of shiny cars, all with
headlights burning strong into the sun.
The black people inside were
as somber as their clothes
and flowers were bright.
After the funeral passed,
we started moving,
and the new breeze
through our windows blew
something more than hope
or loss. I carried my heavy load
into the house of wood and tar paper,
and the husband carried his light one.

Now that you and Max are sleeping,
I'm not ready to go home,
but have pulled over here
off Main Street by this boat ramp
on the Cane to watch this fisherman
come in and this woman's
silver chain of sunfish.

Sportsman's Fucking Paradise

. . . .

Considering some of the serious passion in this poem, one might come to the conclusion that I had progressed beyond being a puppy at this stage, but one might be mistaken, for I would continue to row around on the bayou behind our house, and I would continue to bring fish into it for The Bunny and Christopher, who would be less and less amused, and then to Max, who, from his Johnny-jump-up, would, perhaps, view me and my fish as just another large fascinating shape moving back and forth before him.

And I would become fishin' buddies with an older man who worked in the English Department at the university, a man who made special arrangements with young black women so that they might receive A's in his classes, a man who kept the university president's horses at his ranch so no questions would be asked, a man whose wife carried unexplained bruises, a man who told me as we bobbed on Toledo Bend Reservoir in a bass boat, "I know how it is after the little honey has dropped her calf, so I've fixed you up with a li'l ol' gal in the History Department for a weekend at my cabin."

And I would find this plan so amusing that I would rush home to tell The Bunny so that she might experience the humor, but The Bunny would not find the plan humorous. On the contrary, The Bunny would decide that this man was a dripping piece of pig shit, and the next time I was stupid enough to bring the dripping piece of pig shit into our house, The Bunny would throw dishes at it and would say this to me:

"Get it out of here." And I would escort the dripping piece of pig shit from our house and would never speak to it again.

And one spring day when I would come rowing up to the small landing behind our house, The Bunny would be standing there with a butcher knife in her hand. I would find this particularly engaging because she would be out of her mind on lysergic acid diethylamide and would be strongly suggesting that perhaps this small southern town wasn't conducive to a healthy relationship.

"Get us the fuck out of here."

"Out of where?"

"Out of here, you fucking fuck."

"You don't like our house?"

"I don't like our fucking house, I don't like that fucking little boat you're sitting in, I don't like this fucking university, I don't like this fucking town, and I don't like this fucking state that puts Sportsman's fucking Paradise on its fucking license plates." The Bunny had temporarily forgotten that she was the Queen of Dondore.

News from
the Queen
of Dondore

One day Judy Montgomery Moony Hagerman was sitting up in the branches of a tree behind a Kansas farmhouse eating crackers and jelly. This was one of the only trees for miles and miles, and this was one of the only modes of entertainment for Judy, who had moved to this farmhouse from Brooklyn, New York. And as she ate her crackers and jelly and stared at a solitary tractor kicking up dust perhaps two miles, perhaps five miles away, the tree started talking to her.

"Judy," said the tree, "it appears to me that you are not happy with your circumstances."

"Why would you say that?" said Judy. She was not surprised that the tree was talking to her. Because her stepfather didn't ever talk to her and because her mother, Grace, talked to her too much, Judy had found other, more stimulating, sources of conversation—trees, dogs, horses, grain bins and so on.

"Just a hunch," said the tree.

"Well," said Judy, "we can't do much about that, can we?"

"Oh, but we can," said the tree. "We can transport you to the misty realm of Dondore, where all sorts of powerful and interesting beings will crown you queen and bow down to you."

This plan sounded pretty good to Judy, especially because her other major plan hadn't worked out very well. In that plan, the airplane carrying her favorite baseball team, the Brooklyn Dodgers, would crash near the farm and their famous pitcher,

Sandy Koufax, would be severely injured and would have to stay with her so that she could nurse him back to health. Then he would fall madly in love with her, and they would get married and live happily ever after. Judy was tired of waiting for this to happen.

"OK," said Judy, "the Queen of Dondore it is."

From then on, Judy made a pretty darned good Queen of Dondore. While her stepfather was ignoring her and her mother was talking and talking and talking, the Queen of Dondore was leading her blood-drenched knights through the Chasms of Doom. While Judy was driving a tractor around and around a field for hours without even an umbrella under the scorching sun, the Queen of Dondore was battling enormous bears on the Crags of Percepiton. While Judy's first husband was losing his sanity and drinking himself silly, the Queen of Dondore was making peace between the Legions of Calopine and Shabeezians from the Nether Quadrants. And, of course, when she bore her son, Christopher, he automatically became the Prince of Dondore.

The Queen of Dondore had little difficulty fitting Greg into her scheme of things. After all, he looked quite a bit like a Viking, what with his height, his long blond hair and his propensity for going outside and staying there for a long time. In fact, the staying-there-for-a-long-time part made it easier for her to think of him as the King of Dondore (or at least his stable boy) rather than the genial stumblebum who shared her bed. The Queen of Dondore didn't even mind the fish that Greg brought home and plopped in the sink, for, to her, he was bringing home the heads of Abraxian rebels. Thus when the Queen of Dondore and Greg begat another prince, Max, it was only natural that they should take their princes and move from the Swamp of Despond up into the misty realm of Montana.

An Astonishing
Horizon

. . . .

I wade out into water so fast and clear that I fall in immediately.
How can the Gallatin be this deep here where the stones are so
obvious in their shape and color? I look over where the water
tails out from an undercut bank, and beneath the willow and
alder a whole school of whitefish flashes and drifts sideways
across the pool. I have already lost two Hank Roberts Irre-
sistibles, a deer-hair dry fly that I used to cast to small bass
and bluegill in Oklahoma, because the hair-thin tippets and
tedious blood knots required for this clear water are new to
me. One fly dangles from a willow branch across the river. The
other is in the mouth of something that flashed and tore for the
roots beneath that branch.

Judy, Chris, Max and I have moved from Louisiana to Montana in this late summer of 1975. I have accepted a one-year
appointment in the English Department at the state university
in Bozeman and don't yet know that it will become permanent; I just know that Judy wanted to move and that a year of
trout fishing in Montana might be worth an eternity of rowing
around on the bayou behind our house in Natchitoches.

For the trip up, I drove my VW bug into the U-Haul truck
and tossed our furniture around it. Judy drove her old Ford
Fairlane with Christopher beside her and Max in his port-a-
crib in the back. We hadn't been in our Bozeman four-plex for
two days when Judy said, OK, go, and I drove a few miles to
Gallatin Gateway, parked by a bridge, waded out and fell in.

Across from me, a small gray bird also appears to fall in. But no, it's up on its rock again. What the fuck kind of bird is this, bobbing and cheeping—not falling, just popping in and out of the water. There it goes again. I can see it on the bottom now, strolling around as if the current were a light breeze. Where am I?

I wrap my fly around a twig again, but this time it drops off and rides a small eddy over the deep water beside the upturned roots of a downed cottonwood. I'm not smart enough to wear Polaroids yet, so when I lose track of my fly and try to cast again, I can't because there's a large trout at the end of my line. This fish doesn't dart and flutter, like the ones I'm used to. It swims into the deep, fast water and stays there for a while, then it starts to move, shaking its head, surging then stopping so that I think it's around a rock or log, but then it surges again. I'm surprised that in this clear water I can't see it even when I bring it close. I bend down to get a better look, and it tears out again, ratcheting my crummy reel to a whine.

Because I don't know that I will be in this place for more than a year, I am trying to fix this in my mind, the way the air is already cool even though it's still August, the way the leaves on some of the alders are turning red, the way the distant Bridger Mountains carry an early snow for an astonishing horizon, the way the sky is so blue that it hurts.

Soon the fish turns and I ease it up into the shallows, where I can see that it's a brown trout. What a silly name for a fish that's gold, white, yellow and green, then suddenly purple and turquoise with red spots when I bring it draped sideways on my hand to the surface. Then it flips and is off. Such a gain. What a loss.

Awarded the Court

. . . .

"Hello, young lady," said Wally to Max. "Where's your folks?"

"Hurk, gurk," I said from the tent.

"Unk, urnk," said The Bunny.

"Hello," said Wally, walking toward the tent, "anybody in there?"

"No," I said, pulling on my pants.

"Nobody here," said The Bunny.

This was the early summer of July of 1975. I was back near Trail Creek Pass in Idaho, but this time I was with Judy. Max was bouncing away in his Johnny Jump-Up that hung from a nearby tree, and we were bouncing away in our new orange tent. I was on vacation from my job in Louisiana, Christopher was visiting his father's parents in Kansas, and The Bunny was taking summer classes at Pocatello to finish her doctorate of arts in English. None of us yet knew that we would be in Montana by the end of the summer, so we were making the most of the mountain air. In the midst of the bouncing, Wally, the campground ranger, had pulled up in his ranger truck.

"Oh, I'm sorry," said Wally, gauging the situation as I buckled my belt, "I just wanted to make sure you knew about the bears."

"You mean those bears?" said The Bunny, poking her head from the tent and pointing to the trash barrel that was turned over, with its trash strewn across the camping area.

"Right," said Wally, "I guess you guys already figured that out, huh?"

If only our Wally encounter had been my solitary brush with the law that weekend, but such was not to be the case, for that day I would feel compelled to catch a few small brook trout in the meadow next to us, stuff them in a plastic bag in the foot of my waders, pack some snow around them and bury said waders under our camping gear in the trunk of our car so that the next day we might have a trout dinner with our friends in Pocatello.

On our way back to town, I spotted a sign by a turnout for an Idaho Fish and Wildlife checkpoint. As I pulled into the line of cars to be checked, The Bunny said, "What are you doing?"

"Isn't everyone supposed to pull off here?"

"No," said The Bunny, "only people who are not trying to hide the fact that they have been fishing. I don't think that includes someone who has forgotten to buy a fishing license and has a boot full of fish in his trunk."

"Good afternoon," said the warden, approaching my window.

"Good afternoon, sir," I said. "Sir, I'm afraid that I've pulled off accidentally, sir."

"Oh, really," said the warden. "You mean you haven't been fishing?"

"No, sir," I lied.

"That looks like fishing line hanging from your trunk," said the warden. "Why don't you just step out here and open it up so we can have a little look."

A week later in Pocatello, I was sitting in the court of Justice Christianson. That morning another game warden had knocked on our apartment door, taken me from the arms of The Bunny, driven me around the countryside while he checked some beaver traps, then removed the handcuffs and marched me into the courthouse. I sat there stunned as the judge went through his docket. First came a young Shoshone mother who had been arrested for being publicly intoxicated and urinating in someone's driveway. Judge Christianson talked to her as if she were a little girl.

"Well, Mary, I'm sad to see you here again so soon. We should know better than that by now, shouldn't we?"

"I'm sorry, sir," said Mary. "I'll never do it again."

"But Mary," said Judge Christianson, "isn't that what we said the last time we were here?"

"Yes, sir," said Mary, "but this time I mean it."

"I don't think you do," said Judge Christianson. "I think I'm going to have to help you remember this time by giving you ten days in jail."

"Oh no, sir, please, sir," said Mary. "What about my daughter?" and she looked toward a little girl standing near the entrance with an attendant.

"You should have thought about your daughter before you got drunk," said Judge Christianson. "You should know by now that she will be a ward of the court."

"She will be awarded the court?" said Mary.

"Goodbye, Mary," said Judge Christianson, and Mary and her little girl were led out through separate doors.

"And what have we here?" said Judge Christianson, looking at the piece of paper in front of him and then looking up at me. "How was the fishing?"

"What, sir?" I said.

"How was the fishing, Mr. Keeler?" said Judge Christianson.

"Pretty good, I guess, sir."

"I like to fish too, Mr. Keeler, but I have always struggled through the inconvenience of buying a license. You will pay the court twenty dollars."

"Yes, sir," I said.

"Next," said Judge Christianson.

Later in our apartment, I tried to explain to The Bunny how horrible I felt about watching a woman get separated from her daughter and sent to jail for peeing in a driveway while I just got a slap on the wrist for catching more than the limit of fish without a license.

"Think about it," said The Bunny. "She's an Indian, right?"

"Yes," I said, "but I look like a hippie, what with my long hair and all."

"It might be long, but it's blond, and your skin is pink. You look like a Mormon."

Strictly Academic

. . . .

As a kid growing up in Oklahoma, I had only a vague premonition that there was a dichotomy between fly-fishing and any
other kind of fishing, and that premonition came from Chet
Huntley on the *Huntley-Brinkley Report*. Chet would sometimes end the evening news with a little story or allegory, and
this particular evening it involved fly fishermen and worm
fishermen on the Gallatin River in Montana. I think he was
talking about economics and how ethical corporations lose
out to ones that use underhanded tactics to garner contracts.
He said that this parallels the way that the chances of success
for high-minded fly fishermen fade when evil, greedy worm
fishermen sit by the deep holes near the bridges and catch all
the fish.

I was about fourteen at the time and remember thinking
that Chet must have been stretching things a little because on a
recent trip with my family to the Uncompahgre River in Colo-
rado, I couldn't do for shit on worms but knocked 'em dead
with flies I'd tied with Mother's sewing thread and feathers I'd
pulled from my pillow.

And now I wonder if Chet might be rolling in his grave
because, shortly after his death, Big Sky, a giant skiing resort,
was built near the top of the Gallatin drainage, and its main
lodge was named after him. So now his name is on a place
where hundreds of toilets launch their daily loads toward the
upper Gallatin, and many of these toilets are intermittently
occupied by corporate executives who can afford to stay at
the Huntley Lodge and fish with dry flies near Big Sky Resort

because their companies garnered contracts by using underhanded tactics. It's enough to make a guy go sit under a bridge
and fish with worms.

But it wasn't really until the summer of 1971 when the
department head at Idaho State University was interviewing
me and my friend, Ken Cook, as candidates for their doctor of
arts program that the dichotomy started to flesh itself out.

"And, by the way, Mr. Keeler, do you like to fish?" said Dr.
Stewart.

"That's one of the main reasons I'm here—besides, of course,
your unique course offerings." I wasn't sure what their course
offerings were yet, but I figured that "unique" would cover
most of the bases.

"Oh, really," said Dr. Stewart. "What's your favorite season?"

"For fishing?"

"Yes, for fishing."

"Summer," I said. But actually, I didn't really care when I
fished. I just thought the answer would make me appear more
in tune with the academic calendar.

"I'm a fall man myself," said Dr. Stewart. "The hatches are
fewer and farther between, but when the water warms in the
late afternoon and the browns start surface feeding . . ." His
gaze drifted toward the window. "There's nothing like it, the
low clear water, the backlit aspen, your skin, hot and cold at
the same time, and your fly, say a number fourteen Adams,
drifting on the surface film. Do you understand what I mean,
Mr. Keeler?"

"I sure do," I said. Ken gave me a look because on the previous evening we had caught a large rainbow trout, fishing with
chunks of Velveeta cheese from the dam at nearby American
Falls Reservoir.

"There is nothing that matches casting a dry fly to a rising
brown," said Dr. Stewart.

"Except perhaps," I said, "casting a wet dough ball to a sinking carp." I thought Ken would appreciate the honesty and Dr. Stewart would appreciate the humor. I thought wrong.

"Dough balls?" said Dr. Stewart.

Four years later I was in the office of Dr. Coffin, the head of the English Department here at Montana State University, and I found myself in a similar predicament.

"Do you fish with worms?" said Dr. Coffin.

"Uh, well, uh, I used to. Back in Oklahoma I fished with pretty much everything."

"Everything?"

I was going to try to be funny again and say something like, "Yes, everything—puppies, Alka-Seltzer, WD-40—you know, everything." But recalling how the wet dough balls routine went over with Dr. Stewart, I thought better of it. "But now it's generally just dry flies to rising browns."

"This is good," said Dr. Coffin. "I was afraid you might be a worm fisherman. I would hate to contemplate tenuring one of those."

Thus at the beginning of my career here in Bozeman, my fishing life became inextricably bound to my professional life. When I took my fly rod out on the river, I sometimes felt like a team player and a suck-up. The number fourteen Adams drifting before me in the surface film became, in fact, strictly academic.

When I took my spinning rod out on the river, I frequently felt as if I were risking my career and would slink through the willows and alders with the intensity of a criminal at work.

In either situation, Judy was often my salvation. Though she had long before abandoned any desire to fish with me, her voice would accompany me and mediate many of my internal conflicts.

Greg: OK, so what if I'm fishing maggots with a split shot sinker and a cheap hook I bought at the Pump and Pac convenience mart when I stopped for gas? It's legal, and it's a free country.

Greg's conscience: Nice thinking, Greg, you go right ahead. We don't need to fret about keeping our job here in this pretty little town. We shouldn't worry about what these gas station hooks, sinkers and maggots do to these shiny trout and their fragile little population. And we certainly wouldn't want to tax our little brain with the intricacies of fly-fishing, just to give a few harmless fish more of a sporting chance, now would we?

Greg: Don't you be sarcastic with me, you condescending fuck.

Judy's voice: For all the world cares, you're both just out here wasting your fucking time, so, for Christ's sake, either shut up and fish or get your butts home and do something useful, like clean the house.

A Gerbil Runs
Through It

. . . .

One day in the summer of 1978, I walked into the front office
of the English Department and Norman Maclean, the author
of *A River Runs Through It*, was standing there waiting for Dr.
Coffin to go fishing with him. A couple of summers before,
my friend, Patrick Morrow, had given me a copy of the book,
and I had liked it so much that I shared it with Dr. Coffin, and
Dr. Coffin had liked it so much that he had been instrumental
in inviting Norman Maclean to our campus. So I darted to my
office, grabbed the book and brought it back for him to sign.

I had forgotten that the book had already been inscribed,
twice—once by Patrick Morrow and once by me. Patrick had
written this:

7/18/76
To Gregory Keeler
From the Western American Literature Association
in recognition of outstanding achievement
in the fly-fishing (dry) field.
Awarded by
P. Morrow, Member
Executive Council

I was embarrassed by this inscription, so I put an aster-
isk after "fly" and wrote beneath it in a hand that I thought
resembled Patrick's, "This term, when used in correlation with

Mr. Keeler, is a euphemism for any fish-getting device ranging from dough balls to plastic explosives."

I remembered that I had written this only after I had handed the book to Norman Maclean and he had opened it.

"It looks like several people have already written in here," said Norman. "Who wrote that second part? It's not signed."

"Uh, the guy who wrote the first part," I said.

"Sure, if that's what you say," said Norman. "On a letter scale, how do you rank yourself as a fly fisherman?"

"I guess about a C minus," I said.

"So you've just started fishing with flies?"

"No, I've fished with flies since I was a kid in Oklahoma, and since then I've fished with them in Idaho and Louisiana and now here."

"Well, then, surely you rate above a C minus," said Norman. "I don't want to write that in your book if it's not true."

"It's not that I don't know how to do it," I said. "It's just that I, well, sometimes fish with other kinds of equipment."

"I see," said Norman, and he quickly jotted something in my book and then turned his attention to Dr. Coffin, who had just walked into the office. Here's what he jotted:

June 25, 1978
To Greg Keeler,
From Idaho, Louisiana and Oklahoma,
some stories about Montana
   Norman Maclean

I recount this episode because, though I liked the book, I truly felt like a heap of poop while I read it. After all, Norman's brother, Paul, had, in a sense, died for fly-fishing. And it had been a second religion for his father.

It wasn't until a decade or so later, when the movie came

out, that I fully realized what my bad conscience had bought into. I watched as among the drifting sun-illuminated seed tufts, the glowing mountain scenery and the sounds of water, which had been recorded on rivers throughout America to achieve the perfect gurgle, Robert Redford's noble characters turn Father, Grandma, Granddad, Ralph, Leo, James, Willie Varnum and myself into objects of ridicule.

The only woman on this cinematic river where Norman, Paul and their father fish is a whore who has been hired by an incompetent urban worm fisherman, and everyone is lily-white except for the young Indian woman Paul dates, who seems to be there as a prop to hint at Paul's lifestyle.

I couldn't be mad at Norman for writing in such a lyrical way about his own childhood, but I was hopping mad at Robert Redford for idealizing the values in such a way that his movie lured thousands and thousands of people to Montana, where they bought up much of the land along the pristine rivers while they bought into an illusion of fishing dry flies in a white, patriarchal past.

I was so mad, in fact, that I drove into the Gallatin Canyon, set up a little video camera on its tripod so that it captured the same backdrop where the actor who plays the old Norman is fishing at the end of the movie, and waded around in front of the camera casting and doing my own voice-over, which went something like this:

Hello, I'm Norman McQweeler, and this is *A Gerbil Runs Through It*. We were going to film this scene on the Little Blackfoot, just like in the novel, but mining has poisoned that river with cyanide. We're lucky to be filming it here on the Gallatin River because all of the land around me has been bought up for summer homes. For example, Ted Turner bought up most of the land right over the hill there.

But anyway, when I was a boy growing up in Montana, my father would take us out behind the shed with a metronome, a gerbil, an enema bulb, a gut bucket and a fly rod. . . .

The voice-over stopped here because I slipped on a rock and fell in—which was just as well because as soon as I fell, the woman who, with her husband, owned the adjacent property came down and ran me off. I knew her husband. At the time he was the head of the Bozeman chapter of Trout Unlimited.

A few months later, Judy accidentally erased *A Gerbil Runs Through It*. I guess that was just as well too.

A Fishin' Family

. . . .

Maybe because of my grandparents, part of me always wanted to marry a fishin' woman and have a fishin' family when I grew up, but, for me, fishing was always such an obsession that I never had the patience and rationality to foster such a dream.

During the early Montana years, when I was grappling with my fly-fishing conscience, Judy looked on with mild bemusement from her throne in the realm of Dondore. Earlier in Louisiana, she had accompanied me once or twice on fishing trips, but her interest had waned one day when I was showing her how to cast.

"No, no, Bunny, not like that," I said. "Like this," and I started to gently wrestle the rod from her grip. Before I knew it, The Bunny had thrown down the rod and had grabbed the hair on either side of my head.

"Maybe we don't really need to be fishin' today," said The Bunny through her gritted bunny teeth. She slowly stopped shaking my head and released my hair when she noticed my eyes getting kind of funny and she remembered how large I was.

"Yes," I said, picking up the rod and dusting it off, "maybe we don't."

In Montana, the Queen of Dondore would occasionally descend from her throne to humor me when I was tying flies by suggesting that I might make little tennis shoes for them, or, when I brought a large fish home, she might glance in the sink and say, "My, that one's a real lunker, Greg," somehow making my name sound like an egg salad gone bad. On rare occasions, when she was in a particularly benevolent mood,

I might be practicing my cast in the backyard, and she would grab the end of the line and zigzag around the lawn like a large fish. But mostly, as I've mentioned earlier, she accommodated my solitary fishing sojourns by making sojourns of her own into the realm of Dondore.

In the early summer of 1976, when my one-year appointment at MSU looked like it wasn't going to be renewed and we had sent Christopher to spend some time with his grandparents in Kansas, Judy, Max and I stayed at a cabin next to the river in the Gallatin Canyon. It was a cold, wet June, so while Judy made raging fires in the fireplace and stared into them for hours, I bundled Max up, stuffed him in a backpack thingy and trudged up and down the river fishing. I would sometimes forget he was there until I heard him say "ga" or "wug" when I caught a fish or a wet leaf brushed his face. And when I would bring him back to our cabin and the raging fire, he would say, "Womp," and wobble toward the open arms of the Queen of Dondore.

The next spring, after my contract had been renewed for another year, I took Christopher out fishing in some ponds near Three Forks. As I remember, I was pretty diligent that time. I showed him how to bait up, cast and take the yellow perch off his hook, but he was ten years old by then and had already established his own little realm on the outskirts of Dondore. His heart just wasn't into fishing—unless perhaps in his mind he was hoisting small blood-beasts from the Tarns of Uthrag. I know he was smart enough for such mental exercises, for once when I was arguing with him about a Tuffy trash bag television commercial, he paused and said, "Can't you see, Dad? I'm just playing with you like a little rubber squeezy-duck."

When Max reached that same age of nine or ten, I tried to take him again, this time ice fishing. I decided to make it a special occasion so that he might equate fishing with joyous festivities, so I stopped on our way and bought a bucket of fried chicken. By the time we reached the ice of Canyon Ferry, a reservoir on the Missouri about sixty-five miles from Bozeman, we had consumed most of the chicken and were too bloated and grease-besmeared to care much about catching fish. I had only drilled the first few holes when Max started using them to shoot baskets with chicken bones.

A few years before this, Christopher had discovered Dungeons and Dragons and computers, and now Max was getting into the same set of prerogatives. I remember one particular day when I finally gave up on having anything close to a fishin' family. We all went out to Bracket Creek in the Bridger Mountains to picnic in a meadow. When we arrived, the boys stepped out of the car and said, "What are we supposed to do now?" For a while, they attempted to participate in the setting by tossing a frog back and forth, but then they gave up and sat by the station wagon playing Dungeons and Dragons.

Eventually, whenever I left the house for a lake or stream, Judy would turn to Chris and Max and say, "Don't you want to head out for the ol' fishin' hole with Dad?" Then one of them would say to the other, "Hey, no fair, your cleric can't enter that cave. He's dead 'cause a gas spore killed him," and then, "What did you say, Mom?" And the Queen of Dondore would say, "Nothing."

Dr. Judy and Greg

. . . .

Like many universities in attractive but isolated settings, the one where Judy and I worked in Bozeman has seldom had the tax base to offer competitive salaries, so it depends on its pristine surroundings to secure new faculty. Among faculty who aren't so new any more, this practice is known as eating the scenery. Bozeman's surroundings have always been a bit more enticing to me for obvious reasons and because, as a full-time professor, I have received two to three times Judy's salary for teaching substantially fewer classes. After teaching three classes of freshman composition a semester for twenty-eight years as an adjunct instructor, Dr. Judy's annual take-home pay was around twelve grand when she retired. And as a sort of parting shot, two years before she had to stop teaching because of a chronic disease, the university accidentally took several thousand dollars from her salary, and when Dr. Judy reminded the university of what it had done, it said, "Too late, it's mine now."

Greg: Ummm, this is certainly delicious scenery.
Dr. Judy: Yes, it's not bad—for shit.
Greg: But the mountains and streams are cooked to perfection.
Dr. Judy: If you like shit.
Greg: How about the Big Sky buffet? Surely that can satisfy your appetite?
Dr. Judy: All-you-can-eat shit.
Greg: Those blazing sunsets against the Spanish Peaks, how could you deny that they're the perfect icing on the cake?
Judy: Sugared shit.

Greg: Welp, I guess it's time to go get me another heapin'
helpin' of fishin'.
Judy: Welp, I guess it's time to go get me a big steaming bowl
of shit.

Not that the Great Out of Doors was exactly a continual
banquet for Dr. Greg. Though my father died in 1979, his
spirit lived on when I'd drag the woes of my profession out on
the stream with me. After my dean and his committee denied
me tenure and I was compelled to hire a lawyer in 1980, I went
out to the headwaters of the Missouri for solace, but I found
none. Instead, I broke the tip off of my St. Croix rod trying to
rescue a snagged fly from the top of a bush. In the tradition of
my father, the rest of the rod ceased to be a rod and became a
sack of pig fuck before I sent it whoop-whooping onto the river
from a spot where Lewis and Clark had once camped.

A decade after that, when I had published a book but had
received a minimal reward for doing so, another colleague,
who had promised to publish a book, had received a sub-
stantial reward for not doing so. Thus I drove out to the Yellowstone River, seeking to fish away my woes. But my woes
only increased, for my Pflueger Medalist reel jammed, and an
exceptionally large rainbow trout broke off. Of course, the reel
ceased to be a reel, and became a Christ-forsaken, donkey-
sucking wad of shit-drenched mucus before I found two small
boulders and crushed the reel to a pulp.

How Low
Can You Go?

I have spent many of my hours in Montana fishing in a shameful place. It does not number among the state's sparkling blue-ribbon trout streams. It is not one of the crystalline alpine lakes that dot the state's wilderness areas. No, it is a series of pits dug out for their gravel by bulldozers on Bozeman's outskirts. It is the Bon Ponds. Though these ponds were created before our town's first shopping mall appeared next to them, in my mind they will always be associated with Le Bon Marché (now Macy's), which lies in that mall a few dozen yards across an asphalt parking lot.

And why, over the years, did I spend so much time circling these tawdry pits (now bulldozed into one big pit), when I could have been whipping a fly around in a more sylvan setting? Every year the Department of Fish, Wildlife and Parks lobs several hundred rainbow trout the size of suckling pigs into them. My friend Vern Troxel, a retired logger, first informed me of this virtual stockyard. Initially, I had trouble believing that there were so many trout between five and fifteen pounds free for the taking within the Bozeman city limits, so one evening I drove out to investigate these bleak pits. It was rather difficult to get down to the bank and have a good look because of all of the wild-eyed citizens who had fled their workplaces as soon as the clock would let them. Across the way, it looked like a child had fallen in and his father was trying to pull him from the water, but the huge flailing thing was not a child but a fish. As I shoved my way through the crowd that had assembled around the man, whose shirt had Merl embroidered over his grease-stained pocket, and his now-subdued pig, I noticed that its fins were worn to rounded nubs and its nose was pink and calloused from bumping the concrete walls of hatchery tanks and thought, *How low can you go*?

The last of the sun was turning the sky pink above the distant Madison range that night when I returned to the pits with my own spinning outfit, casting bubble and fly to join the few diehards who hadn't yet caught their pig. A week later, I brought Max, who was around six at the time, and I helped him catch one so big that he decided he didn't want to pull it to the bank for fear it might try to eat him. After I had beat out a little lullaby on its head with a stick, Max decided it was okay to approach it. When he held it up, its tail brushed the ground.

Besides their inordinate size, these pigs helped to sate my appetite for fish flesh without wreaking havoc on the nearby rivers and streams. Eventually I set up an old gutted refrigerator by the alley behind our house, used it as a smoker and kept myself, my friends and my neighbors in smoked fish for years. I would have had a completely clear conscience about this arrangement had it not been for The Bunny, who would sometimes name the huge fish when I plopped them in the sink: "Oh, I see you killed Joyce," or "Are you planning to eat Bob?" or "Looks like Benji got hit by a car."

I won't go into the stories about what it was like to interact with the community of troubled teens, depressed laborers and other habitués of these pits—except for the following:

It was a gloomy fall afternoon, and I had just broken up a dispute between a teenage hooligan and a young mechanic from the nearby Mini Lube. In an act of sheer orneriness, the hooligan had tipped over the coffee can of motor oil where the mechanic had been soaking the corn he was using for bait. Before fishing knives were drawn, I went to my car and found some more motor oil for the mechanic and suggested that the hooligan might expend his energy in a more constructive manner.

No sooner had I returned to casting my plastic bubble and fly than two spiffy lads pulled up behind me in a sports utility vehicle. They both had donned flies in their hats and vests from a recent fishing trip and spoke to me as they might to one who was developmentally challenged.

"'Scuse me," said the tall one, "but isn't this place for kids?"

"Not necessarily," I said.

"Why," said the short one, "would you fish in this puke hole when some of the most pristine water in the country is a few miles from here?"

"Don't know," I said.

"We've been on the upper Missouri," said the tall one. "The rainbows are going nuts on Girdle Bugs. We must have released over twenty, all between two and four pounds."

"Gosh," I said, "you boys must certainly know how to catch them."

"We're not boys," said the short one.

"I wasn't speaking literally," I said.

"You weren't speaking what?" said the tall one.

"Look," said the short one, "he's got one."

And I did have one, a very, very large one. While the drag on my reel screamed, it started moving toward the other end of the pond, seemingly unaware that it was hooked.

"Jesus," said the tall one.

"You should set your drag tighter," said the short one.

"No," said the tall one, "leave it loose."

"Can I hold your rod for a minute?" said the short one.

"No," I said.

After about fifteen minutes, the twelve-pound pig was wallowing around near shore and the short one fell in trying to wrestle it out of the water. Before they left, they asked me to take their picture while, with one hand, they held the fish between them, and, with the other, they held their fly rods.

Stink Meat

- -

But the depravity of the Bon Ponds pales next to an indignity I forced upon myself on the lower Yellowstone at a community so aptly named Intake, Montana. The travesty commenced one spring in the early nineties, when I beheld a photo in a regional fish and game tabloid of a gentleman in a Harley Davidson baseball cap hoisting a gargantuan shark-like fish with a proboscis longer than its head. In the crook of his arm nestled a deep-sea fishing rod and reel with a spark plug and a giant treble hook dangling from the line. Enthralled, I read on.

I discovered that it was a paddlefish, and the motorcycle aficionado was using a spark plug and a treble hook because the behemoths only feed by filtering plankton through their gills; thus, to catch one on fishing tackle, one must snag it. As instructed by the article, I proceeded to the Department of Fish, Wildlife and Parks to buy my paddlefish-snagging license and tag. In the accompanying instruction pamphlet, I gleaned that a fossil of one of these fish had been excavated from within the ribs of a duck-billed dinosaur.

That weekend, I was supposed to meet my friends Ed and Jenny Dorn and Dobro Dick at the Wild Horse Pavilion, a whorehouse in Miles City, Montana. From there, we were to launch forth into the phantasm of the Miles City Bucking Horse Sale, but with my new deep-sea fishing rig gleaming in the back of my pickup, I only stopped long enough in Miles City to silently mouth, "Nope, they're not here," and then sped on to the irrigation dam at Intake.

Arriving at such a place, one might at first think that one had come upon a grotesque backwoods religious ritual. For approximately two hundred feet stretched a line of men, women and children dressed in costumes ranging from rompers to leisure suits to bikinis, all holding the requisite deep-sea fishing rig, spark plug, and treble hook, awaiting their turn at the head of the line to snag a paddlefish and then proceeding to the back of the line, passing their rod over the heads of those who would follow them.

Without wasting a second, I secured my place among their ranks and waited my turn. On the bank not far behind us sat families with blankets and picnic baskets, and between those waiting and casting and those picnicking raced children and dogs. Occasionally I would hear a screech or a whoop as a spark plug beaned a child or a treble hook snagged a dog. The paddlefish were so plentiful, backed up where they could continue no farther because of the irrigation dam, that it was no time at all before I was at the front of the line snagging my own and then working my way over the heads of fellow anglers to the back.

As I battled the anachronism, I could tell that it was large, but it tuckered quickly, and I dragged it to shore next to an adolescent girl, sunburned in her pink terry cloth short shorts and a T-shirt that said Daddy's Little Girl. Her daddy, a huge darkly tanned fellow in an AC/DC T-shirt with the sleeves torn off, was weighing her fish, still hooked to her line. "Twenty-five pounds," he bellowed.

"Mine's twenty-five pounds. How big is yours?" said the girl.

"I don't know," I said.

"Daddy," said the girl, "come here and weigh this guy's fish."

As I pulled it quivering up on the rocks, the man said, "Hell, it's just a dink, sixteen pounds at the most. I ain't even gonna weigh it."

"Yours is just a dink," said the girl.

"And look," said Daddy, "it's been caught before. See that

hole there where somebody took their tag out? I guess they must've upgraded. You'd best keep that there dink 'cause it ain't gonna live much longer nohow."

"I was planning on it," I said.

"You'd best," said Daddy, "and you'd best gut it out quick 'cause they don't last long in this heat. That there's the guttin' shack." He pointed to a building that was hardly more than a booth in a nearby clump of cottonwoods.

Standing in the gutting shack, nursing an ice-cold Bubble-Up and inspecting my catch where it lay gleaming on a slab by the cleaning sink before me, I began to have reservations. This creature wasn't grotesque; it was cartoon-like. For want of a better word, it was cute, what with its beady little eyes, its long flat nose and its blimp-like body. It somehow reminded me of the Hudson my parents owned when I was a toddler. Its ancestors had swum with the dinosaurs, and I had dragged it into my world to be labeled a dink and lugged to the gutting shack.

I looked out the window, which was more of a big rectangular hole in the wall with its cover propped open on a stick. Just outside was a large Dumpster filled with the heads and guts of paddlefish. An Asiatic fellow was furtively going through the guts, sorting out the strips of caviar and slipping them into a large red cooler beside him. I don't think such a practice had yet been banned, but, by his discreet behavior, I assumed that it was discouraged.

My heart sank as I gazed upon all those severed heads with their beady little eyes and comic bills, so I quickly plopped my own contribution on top of the pile, gutted the body, slabbed it into steaks, carved off the strong-smelling meat on the periphery of each one, tossed the refined product into my cooler on some ice among my remaining Bubble-Ups and toted it to my pickup. As I loaded it in the back, Daddy's Little Girl approached me.

"Got your dink in there?"

"What's left of it," I said.

"Djew cut the stink-meat off it?" she said, tugging at her shorts where they had sunk into her crotch.

"Yes, I did," I said.

"Lemme see." She reached in and started to lift the lid of the cooler.

"Sorry, but I have to go now," I said, swinging up the tailgate.

"Daddy," yelled the girl toward a camper across the parking lot. "This guy didn't cut the stink meat off his dink."

"He what?" yelled Daddy, hefting his bulk from the back of the camper. I didn't hear what else he said because, by the time he was across the parking lot, I was on my way back to Bozeman where, upon viewing the remains of my paddlefish, The Bunny said, "Where's the rest of Debbie?"

Is He Fishing?

It is 1962 and I'm in a hospital in Enid, Oklahoma. I'm fifteen
years old and have come to visit Granddad. The nurse won't
let me into the room, but Granddad sees me in the hall and
raises a hand and says, "Hi, Bub." The hand is huge and swollen, with a tube running into the wrist below it. The nurse
missed the vein with the IV, so the plasma has gone into the
rest of the hand. It looks like Mickey Mouse's hand, it is so big.
It doesn't look much like the hand that cut up roadkill for the
trotlines or covered my hand when it was teaching me to fish
with a cane pole. The nurse closes the door, and I never see
Granddad again.

The doctors have found a cancer that has grown for years in
his prostate. Grandma told me that the doctors said it was so
big and there was so much of it that it looked like fat spaghetti.
I'm wishing she hadn't shared that with me, because now I'm
picturing something that Granddad probably would have used
for bait

And now it is Christmas of 1978, and I'm thirty-two. I have
flown from Montana to be here in the bedroom of my parents'
new house on the outskirts of Stillwater, Oklahoma. There is
a large pond behind the house, and I have been fishing in it
because Father is inside dying of cancer and I don't know what
else to do. Sometimes Mother will come down to the pond and
say, "Are you catching anything?" and I will say, "Yes, Mom,
they're biting pretty good," and she will stand there watching
me because she doesn't know what else to do either.

The day before this one, she went down to where I was

fishing and said, "I have to leave for a while, so will you come in and keep an eye on your father. He may wake up and ask you to give him these pain pills. If he does, please don't give them to him. When he was thinking clearly, he told me that too many of them make him feel crazy, and he would rather feel the pain than feel crazy."

An hour after Mother left, Father woke up and came into the recreation room where I was watching a rerun of *Leave It to Beaver* on the television.

"Where are the pain pills?" said Father.

"I have them, Dad. They're right here," I said, and I handed him the pain pills.

And now, here in this bedroom, I am telling Father that I have to go back to Montana because the classes I am teaching will start in two days. I am trying to think of a way to say goodbye because I know I will never see Father again, so I say something really stupid.

I say, "Welp, Dad, I guess it's about time for the big guy to be flying off to Montana."

For this occasion, Father has pulled himself out of his pain for a moment of complete clarity that would, under normal circumstances, be common for this fifty-nine-year-old English professor who is known for his dark wit.

"Welp, son," says Father, "I guess it's about time for the shriveled guy to be flying into the ground."

To a Father Long Gone

Who could escape into the life of a sunfish
without becoming a slave to imagery? Green,
longear, pumpkinseed, bluegill, warmouth—wish
for the distant years where youth made these mean
little but joy, and you find yourself trapped behind
bars that come and go by instinct in rushes

of fear or weather. Long to color a mind
long lost to abstraction, and a bright orange blushes
behind a turquoise so deep you could slip on a thought
and kill yourself. Better to stick with a father
and watch the bobber dive, on a deep life caught,
from red and white to dark green than bother
to go there now, a father yourself, alone in a boat,
the sunfish a hidden mystery, colored by hope.

A month later, I find myself in a room in the Stillwater hospital, sitting beside my grandmother, who is also dying of cancer. I have spent the evening lifting her from her bed to the
toilet and back.

"Gotta go, gotta go," says Grandma. Her urgency may be
due to the fact that the cancer in her liver has grown so much
that it is crowding out her other organs, including her urinary
bladder, but, more likely, it is due to the fact that she knows she
is dying and wants to be held as much as possible before she
goes. I am still too close to these events to allow myself to see
the various ironies involving the decline of this strong woman
who taught me the practical value of using chicken livers and
chicken guts for bait, who is now blurring the boundaries
between going to the bathroom and going to her death.

"Gotta go, gotta go," says Grandma.

And now it is April 2001 and I am again in Stillwater, sitting
beside Mother in her house by the pond. Again, I have been
fishing, but this time, because Mother is the one who is dying,
she has not been able to walk down to the pond and ask me if
I'm catching anything. Instead, she has occasionally asked my
stepfather, Frank, "Is he fishing?" and Frank has said, "Yes,"
and she has responded, "Good."

I did not want to come to watch my mother die of cancer because I had heard that she was not in her right mind

and would not recognize me if I came, but two days ago, my phone rang in Montana and it was Mother, and she said in a deep, beyond-the-grave voice not unlike that of Vincent Price, "Greg, why aren't you here? I am ready to die."

And now here on her deathbed, before a sliding glass door through which she can look out on the sky, she has gathered what remains of her immediate family and has pulled herself together to try to laugh at our jokes and listen to us sing her favorite songs. Before I go to my motel for the night, Frank leans down next to Mother and tells her that she is going to a better place, and she, who has been a Methodist disciple of Jesus all her life, looks out where the sky and the pond are turning red under a setting sun and says in her Vincent Price voice, "I'm not so sure about that."

The next morning, when my brother, Ted, calls and tells me that Mother has died in the night, I will get in his car and start driving toward the house, but I will have to stop and pull over because, even though I will never come to any conclusions about the existence of a god, I will see a sunrise that will make it hard for me to breathe or swallow or think.

On a Lighter Note

Fortunately for my equipment, my family and my head, I have found a fishing friend who helped take my mind off my losses and put it more directly on the sport at hand. Vern Troxel has combined my fishing past and present. He has been a blend of Granddad, Grandma, Father, Ralph and Leo. Vern is a retired logger I met in the mid-seventies at a gathering of high school and college English teachers hosted by his wife, Joann, a teacher at Bozeman Senior High School. I was trying to make small talk about the horrors of collaborative learning when a gnome-like man walked into the room with a mug of home brew and a platter of giant smoked trout. That was all it took. I spent the next twenty years with Vern—spin fishing, bait fishing, fly-fishing and more particularly, ice fishing for perch—so many perch that The Bunny gave up trying to name them all. Vern got me so addicted to this practice that, when his body finally started to fail him in the mid-nineties, I wrote him this tribute and published it in the 1994–1995 winter issue of *Big Sky Journal*.

In a Perch's Eye

. . . .

Time to get the tip ups out of the garage and replace the diminutive Mr. Twisters and Sassy Shads; time to tie on the Dicky Pearls and polish off the Swedish Pimples; time to string up some new line.

On Canyon Ferry, they let you fish six lines through the ice, so winter can be a real meat fest, especially if you like perch. Vern Troxel does. Vern and I have haunted that first major reservoir on the Missouri near Townsend for about twenty years, ever since he first showed me how to pop a perch's eye from its head, poke it on a barb and catch another perch with it. In the fifties, Vern moved to Townsend from Wisconsin for the logging. In Wisconsin, they know a lot about perch. Vern can wander out to a spot on a vast plane of ice, say "here," drill a hole and catch perch until his Styrofoam cooler cracks.

I've watched him closely to see what he does. There's a dance involved—having to do with the auger—where he takes his time drilling and stares off toward Mount Baldy while humming some obscure song from the fifties. There are also certain subtle movements, but since Vern is a small man and since his legs have been mangled so badly over the years by broken saw chains and fallen trees, the subtleties are hard to pick out from his normal stance. There is also the elixir of his home brew that adds communion to the dance with a dark rich flavor, a mood of color and temperature that seems distilled from an essence lying deep under the ice. Somewhere in this process, he points his rod to a spot two and a half inches above the hole; then, as if charged by some small voltage below, his arm will go up, the wand will bend and he will add another fish to the flopping pile that has materialized beside him.

Sometimes, after the ice is thick enough to drive on, a pickup will pass, and Vern will decipher the primitive code of its bellowing driver: "Vince says they're takin' hawgs near the dikes." This means we will soon be at the shallow end of the lake, lifting perch the size of acorn squash from three feet of water, building small bunkers around ourselves with their bodies. I'm always rather astounded that so many huge perch would rush to a single spot where they've just seen several colleagues jerked into oblivion. Vern just takes it as a matter of course as he heads and guts them with a couple of strokes of his knife, pops a few of their eyes out and baits up again.

At this point, squeamish readers may be flinching from the carnage, but I must beg your indulgence. There's a point. Perch taste good.

If there were a Norman Rockwell painting of a gawking, bug-eyed, flat-topped boy scarfing down fried fish, I would be that boy, and perch fillets would be that fish. A fellow from Fish and Wildlife who lives down the street from me will drive straight home from the lake and single-handedly eat his whole catch in one sitting. Vern goes into a Wisconsin lilt when he talks of preparing them for the table—flour-dusted, beer-battered, blackened, broiled or boiled and buttered; close to but better than walleye. He'll fillet fifty to a hundred in a night, zipping the knife down the spine, around the rib cage and under the skin—as if he's conducting a little meat symphony, parceling out every flake of flesh like an expensive, illicit drug.

Sometimes Vern can't go with me, and my perching trips devolve into tawdriness. The ritual dancing, singing and bellowing vanish, and I'm left in an existential void. Instead of heading straight through a blizzard for the ice, sixty-five miles from Bozeman, I'll let the snow distract me and pull in at a truck stop in Belgrade. There I'll order "the brain eater," a combination of biscuits and gravy that resembles a chunky viscous fluid from an old science fiction movie of the same title.

When I arrive at the lake, I'll let various local phenomena distract me from the ritual at hand. Instead of singing and staring at Mount Baldy, I'll watch snow-suited East Helenans whizzing across the ice on ATVs, pink-cheeked toddlers perched on their gas tanks serving as windbreaks, while I drink Old Milwaukee tall boys. I will slip and hit my head on the ice so that the afternoon becomes an odd dream—not a nightmare, but more of a quandary: There used to be perch here. I saw them. Vern showed them to me.

I will imagine how, in Vern's presence, a cloud of perch the size and shape of a '56 Buick will pull up under his feet and debark through the hole before him. Without Vern, the Buick never arrives. By two or three o'clock, the "brain eater" and the tall boys will make me question whether the five perch I've caught are real or just reminiscences.

I will enter a sort of surreal realm where perch are replaced by an Oriental dragon fish called ling or bourbot, a fish designed to eat things larger than its head with a mouth that expands into an aquatic Hoover, a Hoover that vacuums up perch. Years ago, Vern used to describe ling as a vague possibility, something that lived in Clark Canyon Reservoir near Dillon and tasted like rattlesnake, something that could be caught at night with treble hooks buried in balls of dog food. But in recent years, they have exponentialized in Canyon Ferry. Without Vern beside me, the ling creep up like Gothic chimeras, chasing and eating all the prettier fish and then gulping the eye dangling on my Swedish Pimple so that I have to snakeease them up through the hole and watch them vomit schools of small perch on the ice before me.

It seems that the less Vern is able to accompany me, the more the ling reproduce and diminish the perch. I've grown to view this conflict in terms of *Star Wars*, with Vern as Yoda, the ling as Darth Vader and Vern's home brew as "The Force." When one of their horrid devil's heads breaches in the hole before me, I feel Vern materializing over my shoulder, chanting, "Use the Brew, Greg. Don't give in to the ling side." Thus, graphite light saber in one hand and dusky brown bottle in the other, I quaff the elixir and do battle with the forces of darkness.

The Poetry of Failure:
A Bobber, a Song
and a Dead Porcupine

. . . .

Who knows why the combination of nature and nurture so frequently leads anglers to write poetry and poets to go fishing, but during my years in Bozeman, I have often found myself on the stream with poets. In the fall of 1978, I wrote a letter to the Missoula poet Richard Hugo, who many still consider to be the literary soul of Montana, inviting him down to Bozeman to fish and give a reading at MSU. He responded immediately, saying that he'd been wanting to come to Bozeman for a long time, so the following spring, after several more exchanges concerning both poetry and fishing, he wrote the following:

> April 1, 1979
> *Dear Greg:*
> Well, it turns out I'll probably come down on Saturday or Sunday, and stay with a friend. We have in mind fishing a private pond on Monday and depending on conditions, possibly the creek on Tuesday or maybe that too on Monday. Of course if I come down on Saturday, we may hit the pond Sunday. You're invited, absolutely. . . . We'll need worms—anyway, I'll need worms, being a crudebait fisherman, unchanged after 55 years, unredeemed, but trying to overcome my crassness with charm.
> Warmly,
> Dick

P.S. Greg, a switch in plans. If I can stay with you, OK. If not I'll take a motel. My friend can't come now, but fishing is on, both in the pond and in the creek, if water conditions permit.

Dick's letter got me revved up on several levels. I was tickled that he wanted to fish with me, and my Oklahoma blood had been yearning for some good ol' bait fishing. Since Hugo poems are full of ideal ponds and streams, somehow the word "private" in his letter created a picture of the *perfect spot* in my mind, a stream in a dark forest with sun angling through to illuminate deep, trout-filled pools. I was also struck by the humility and self-deprecation I'd become so familiar with in his poetry, a humility that is frequently bound to the notion that failure is success and vice versa. From the confusion of his letter, I should have known that our sojourn might lead to something less than a *perfect spot* and, in the terms of his poetry, meet with raging success.

Though I'd heard that Dick was on the wagon, he was barely out of his pickup in front of our house when he had me gunning it down to the liquor store for a bottle of Early Times. Over a few whiskey ditches, he told me that he couldn't stand any kind of elitism in angling and liked to sit in a lawn chair next to a pond or lake, fishing with worms and a huge bobber that went *whok* when it hit the water, "happy as a pig in shit." All of this put me at ease since Dick reminded me so much of my recently deceased father, also a World War II vet who fished with bait and used profanity with elegant precision.

The next morning I remember being a little apprehensive unloading our gear from the back of Dick's pickup when he hefted out a folding lawn chair and stuck it under his arm. Though he was a strong and burly man, he was also pretty, well, rotund, and from what I gathered, walking was not among his major interests. The "trout stream" turned out to be little more than a turbid trickle, so we decided to hike to the pond. Dick's friend had told him that it was "just over the hill," but neither of us was quite sure what that meant in native-speak. We found out the hard way.

"Damn, Keeler, I'd swear he said it was just over the hill," said Dick, huffing and puffing and hobbling because of a childhood hip injury from a bicycle accident.

"I'll run up over the next hill," I said, "and see if it's there."

"OK," said Dick. "I'll have a smoke in my chair." So he unfolded his chair, whipped out a Benson and Hedges and proceeded to smoke between his huffing and puffing.

I finally found what a Munchkin might call a pond, little more than a pool with a hurricane fence around it about half a mile (and two hills) over. When I returned to break the bad news to Dick, he had left his lawn chair and was standing over something, smoking another Benson and Hedges and mumbling.

"Gawd, who in the hell would do a thing like this?"

"What?" I said peering over his shoulder.

"This," and he pointed to a dead porcupine in front of him with a hole in its head.

"Maybe it nailed somebody's dog and they got pissed," I said, trying to provide him with a rational answer, though Dick wasn't really looking for answers.

"I mean, for Christ's sake, who would shoot a fucking porcupine? I can see the headline, PORCUPINE TERRORIZES COMMUNITY, MUST BE PUT UNDER."

Still trying to find logic in the situation, I said, "Some of the guys around here just like to go out and 'shoot stuff.'"

"Let's get the hell out of here," said Dick. "Did you find that lake?"

"Yes," I said, "but it's more of a little fenced-in pool than a lake."

"Maybe my friend has been too busy shooting stuff to notice the difference between a lake and a puddle," said Dick.

As he was loading his lawn chair into the back of the truck, he said, "Where's that whiskey?"

That evening after dinner and many shots of Early Times, I found out that Dick wasn't too fond of smart-asses when I picked up my guitar and played him a song I had written called "Latter Day Worm Fisherman," based on a concept I ripped off from Milford Poltroon's *How to Fish Good.* I think the part of the song that he found of particular interest went as follows:

As I was ridin' down to the Railroad Ranch last weekend,
The road was all lined up with Utah license plates.
A lot of funny little guys was wadin' in the water,
Fishin' wiff they fly rods like the sign said that they oughtta,
But when I got close up, they was usin' worms for bait.

Dick said, "That's very funny, Keeler, play it again." So I played it again, and Dick said, "That's very funny, Keeler, play it again." So I played it again, and Dick said, "That's very funny, Keeler, play it again." While I was playing it for about the fifth time, I paused when I heard an odd noise that my wife, Judy, later described as sounding like someone beating a ham against the side of a bathtub. Dick said, "Oh, excuse me, I seem to have farted, but where were we—oh yes, that's very funny, Keeler, play it again."

The next evening when Dick gave his reading to a large, responsive audience, I was amazed at how the poems seemed like an elegant extension of his normal conversation, how he took the audience into his confidence in the same way that he had made me feel like an old friend in the three days that I had known him.

Over the next couple of years, Dick and I had several more successful failures at fishing, and in the spring of 1982, when he came over with his wife, Ripley, to receive an honorary doctorate that I had helped to nominate him for, we went fishing one last time. Though he died of cancer that fall, I still feel his warmth, humor and compassion every time I pick up a book of his poetry, and, to this day, I never play "Latter Day Worm Fisherman" without hearing, "That's very funny, Keeler, play it again."

Don't Move

Once, in the early eighties, I found myself fishing on the West Gallatin with Gary Snyder, the poet of Zen Buddhism and the American West. Over the years, Gary has asked me to perform my songs with him at various literary and environmental functions, and if any single person (besides The Bunny and my parents) has had a clear effect on the way I live my life, it is Gary and his main dictum: Don't move. That is, live in one place—learn the land, the water, the plants and the animals of that place, become part of its story and make it part of yours.

On this particular fishing trip, I was trying to impress Gary with my knowledge of the place, and thought I was succeeding fairly well when we stopped for lunch and were eating some smoked rainbow trout that I had caught on a previous fishing trip.

"Tell me, Greg," said Gary, "Are there any nutrients in the skin of this trout?"

"Uh, yes, uh, there are plenty," I said, not having the foggiest notion but eating some of the wretched-tasting skin just to show that I knew what I was talking about.

"And what brings you to this conclusion?" said Gary, watching with interest as I gagged on some belly skin.

"Uh, well, uh, you know how many of a potato's nutrients are in its skin?"

"Yes."

"Well, it's sort of like that with trout."

"So the trout is a distant relative of the potato?"

"Sort of."

"And here I've been thinking all along," said Gary, "that fish skin was mostly just fat."

It sometimes took me a little while to realize when Gary was kidding me, though I should have figured it out when, early in our friendship, he handed me a little card that made sport of North Dakotans. On one side it said, "How do you keep a North Dakotan busy all day?" and at the bottom of the card it said "(Over)." Then on the other side of the card, it said, "How do you keep a North Dakotan busy all day?" and at the bottom of the card, it said, "(Over)."

After I finished choking down the rest of the trout skin, we fished where the river flows through the Flying D (now Ted Turner's) Ranch. As usual, I became so involved in catching fish that I lost track of everything else. About an hour later, I looked up the bank, but Gary wasn't there, and I thought, oh no, he got pissed off at me and has gone back to the car. But when I got to the car, he wasn't there either. So in this pristine setting, I disrupted the sounds of the river and the wind through cottonwood leaves as I dashed up and down the bank, yelling, "Gary, Gary."

After a while he walked up behind me, seemingly from out of nowhere, with a cottonwood leaf in his hair.

"Yes?" said Gary.

"I, I thought you were lost," I said.

"I was just trying to take a little nap." He put only the slightest emphasis on the word "trying." "It would be difficult to be lost in a place like this."

"Yes," I said, "I guess it would."

Later that evening at our house before dinner, Gary wrote this in my copy of his book, *The Old Ways*:

> *For Greg and Judy Keeler*
> After a day out fishing on the Gallatin
> at the "Flying D"—cottonwood leaf
> in the hair—beer in the irrigation
> ditch—warm late summer day
>   Gary S.

My fishing encounters with Gary always seemed to involve poetry. Once, in 1983, my friend Brad Donovan and I drove over to fish for steelhead on the Clearwater River near Lewiston, Idaho. After the first day of being skunked, we checked into a motel and went to Keith and Shirley Browning's house that evening. Keith is a literary institution at the college there, and the Alaskan poet John Haines was giving a poetry reading in his basement. Somehow, that evening of poems about the Alaskan wilderness, moose bones, wood smoke and salmon seemed to invest us with the spirit of success. The next day, we headed straight for a turnoff called Coyote's Fishnet, and I caught a ten-pound steelhead.

At Keith's house, we had heard that Gary was giving a reading a few miles north at the University of Idaho in Moscow, so we iced up the steelhead in our cooler, checked into a motel, tromped up to campus and stumbled right into Gary. On the spur of the moment, he asked me to play some songs as a warm-up for his reading that evening, and I gladly obliged. Ron McFarland, the professor who had arranged the reading, wasn't too thrilled about these arrangements since they had paid good money for Gary and I was just some bumpkin eating into his time, but the audience seemed to like the combination.

Gary and I had made these last-minute arrangements at other performances too, once in Missoula where the audience assumed I was some kind of joke Gary was playing on them, and once in West Yellowstone for the Greater Yellowstone Coalition, where Chip Rawlins, a Wyoming writer, kept making the cut-it signal with his finger across his throat to get me to stop so Gary could start.

But there in Moscow, the audience seemed to appreciate both of us, and the next morning we had a pancake breakfast at the motel restaurant. Afterward we showed Gary the cooler of steelhead fillets.

"Is it wild or hatchery?" said Gary.

"Uh, I think it's wild. Its fins were in good shape when I landed it."

"And that means it's wild?" said Gary.

I had experienced this line of questioning before concerning the skin of a smoked fish. "Actually," I said, "I don't have a clue."

Just as our fishing encounters usually involved poetry, my poetry encounters with Gary frequently involved fishing. In the early nineties, he invited me down to the University of California at Davis to give an evening performance and to join him in teaching his workshop in writing poetry. In an attempt to show the class my "poetics," I read them the following poem:

Ode to Rough Fish

I speak for the carp, fat on mud-bloat
and algae, orange-lipped lipper of algae surfaces,
round rotter of the banks of hydroelectric rivers.
Not the quick thin-meated trout
darting his pretty life in the rare rocks of high streams.

Ah, and the rooting sucker, round, tubed mouth
    distended
to bobble rocks, worms, offal, whatever
he can turn up without himself turning up.

Yes, here's to you, scum-suckers of the stagnant
reservoirs and sludge-filled rivers, livers on
waste discharge, suckers down of anything we can
slop on you at our worst moments.

Long live you who will live long whether
we say so or not, who would as soon wallow in

the hollow of a bloated, river-soaked moose corpse
as live up to a size 20 Coachman on a 7X tippet.
You live up to nothing, and we will never live you down,
for you horrid-mouthed mouthers of death and
worse than death have found something stronger
than the slats of your hard flat scales.

Where a trout jumps for the thin wings of a fresh-
hatched caddis, you jump for nothing but air
through the filth and oil slicks.
Where a trout darts at a nymph behind a rock, you
could care less; you move the sonofabitching rock
and all the mud around it. Yes, you too will
find the nymph and eat it, but you will also eat
the mud and love it.
Yes, you love mud.
Mud is your guts; thus, your guts are always distended
in thick slabs of carp meat—sucker meat.
You and your wallowing, blubbery truth.
You and your truth that has made a heaven of sewage.
Why didn't they call you rainbow or golden,
for if God gave a promise and a warning
in one fell swoop,
you are it.

Later, I read about the class in an essay called *The Poet in the
University* that Jack Hicks wrote for *Gary Snyder: Dimensions of
a Life*, and Gary and his students had decided that my poetics
involved "suckers" and "whackers." Suckers are poems that
suck the audience in and subvert their preconceptions, while
whackers are poems that beat the audience over the head with
their message. I'm hoping they thought "Ode to Rough Fish"
was a sucker.

Fishing with
Captain Colossal

. . . .

But of all the poets and writers I accompanied on the lakes and streams around Bozeman, I probably spent the most time with Richard Brautigan, or the Captain, as I came to call him. So much time, in fact, that I wrote a book about it called *Waltzing with the Captain: Remembering Richard Brautigan*. The book concerns our friendship between the time I met him in 1978 and the time of his suicide in 1984. Here's the chapter about fishing:

For the Captain, fishing was usually past or future tense. The equipment, the flies, etc., were in the present. He had a glass rod, light as a weed, and he liked to hold it out and shake it slightly, then pass it to the person next to him to experience the proper awe. The flies he used were also next to nothing, size sixteen to twenty. Most of the time, this wonderful tackle sat unused in the washroom.

But there were those rare occasions when we would actually put the equipment in the back of my Mazda station wagon and go out to a local stream. One such excursion was to the Yellowstone, about a mile behind Richard's house. He was in a twinkling mood because he had just sold the option on *Dreaming of Babylon* to Kate Jackson. Maybe that and the cool, clear weather got him out from behind the Dickel, into my car and down a dirt road to the river. Taking his stuff out of the back, he hit his head on the swing-up tailgate so that he bled a little. But it didn't seem to faze him. As we squeaked and wallowed down the bank in our huge, clown-like chest waders, we commented on what the Japanese must have intended when they built cars with tailgates like that and sold them to big lumbering Americans.

Richard waded upstream and fished the slower water inside a big riffle on a bend in the river with a tiny dark nymph. I waded downstream a ways where the water was straight and fast and lobbed a big spoon toward the deep blue-green near the undercut of the far bank. Richard looked down at me from where he was fishing. He never fished with anything but flies—at least as an adult. Once he told me that he used to fish salmon eggs to carp where the sewage came into a river in Tacoma. He said he could actually see flecks of toilet paper among the wallowing carp. But apparently he had left that kind of behavior behind with his youth, or maybe that was the only part of his youth that he had left behind. Actually, fishing salmon eggs to toilet paper carp still sounds pretty good to me. I've never gotten over my childish infatuation with bait and lures, though I'll fish with flies if they happen to be working better.

After a while, the Captain caught a couple of nice whitefish. Local fishermen usually throw whitefish up on the bank and let them rot, but not Richard. He had seen too many of them smoked and selling for five dollars a pound in the Bay area. He had also seen Japanese friends go ape shit when they got their hands on a whitefish. No sir, these whitefish were immediately cleaned and popped in my creel that I had left up on the bank near him. He called my creel the "Death Bag" since he knew how much meat had passed through it. Soon, I was fooling some rainbow trout in the deep water with my big hunk of metal. Since I didn't have my creel, I just threw them up on the bank in a sort of frenzy. After a while, I turned to deal with the flopping fish, but Richard was already there, clonking each fish very precisely on the head with a small rock. "You should kill them quickly," he said with a smile of mild accusation.

Later, I filleted the trout and Richard put the whitefish in for smoking. I have a smoker in my backyard made from a converted refrigerator. Richard called it Auschwitz. Smoked fish were always an integral part of our relationship. Sometimes he'd have me send boxes of smoked fish express mail to people like Shiina Takako, his Japanese sister in Tokyo, or Terry Gardiner, the "wild legislator" in Ketchikan, Alaska. And sometimes that worked out pretty well for me. Once Shiina Takako sent me a box of ayu, a rare Japanese fish, preserved in a delicate oil. But Terry Gardiner never responded. I have a feeling that he might have come home from some political junket to find a package of smoked trout rotting in his mailbox.

Perhaps the most idyllic trip we ever took was to Bridger Creek, just outside Bozeman city limits. Richard really liked small streams, maybe because they seemed more magical, and the fish that come out of these streams are almost always harder, crisper and brighter in color. We waded just upstream from a small irrigation dam and started flailing. This time, Richard had shamed me into bringing my fly rod, so we were more or less on even footing. Richard was using about a size eighteen white gnat-like fly, and I was using some crude thing I'd made by tying frazzled chunks of nylon to small hooks, but the fish didn't seem to care what we threw at them. They were so hungry we probably would have done pretty well using rabbit shit. We must have caught and released ten or fifteen fish apiece (yes, I said "released"; Richard shamed me into that too) before the landowner came down and ran us off. Richard may have had his way on using flies and releasing fish, but I still managed to drag him into one of my foul fishing practices. As we left, he said, "You see, Greggie, you're supposed to ask permission," in a tone quite similar to the previous, "You should kill them quickly."

But as I mentioned in starting, most of my fishing trips with the Captain had very little to do with fishing. They usually went something like this: Richard would call me around nine or ten in the morning and say, "Let's go fishing." Since he knew that I was always suspicious of this midmorning suggestion, he would throw in something like "I know the perfect spot on Trail Creek" or "Go ahead and bring some sculpins too. I won't mind." And when he knew he had my interest, he would say, "Oh, and on your way, stop and buy some George Dickel. I'll pay you back."

Of all these suggestions, usually the only one that transpired was my buying the Dickel. When I got to the ranch, the Dickel would be opened for "just a quick snort for the road." But soon the road would lead into long painful discussions of his divorce, his water rights, the teenagers who had "vandalized" his barn, the black hole where money-grubbing publishers live, the question of whether or not to marry Masako and have a hit squad of Japanese-American kids, the doppelganger cat that had invaded his ranch, the mutant potatoes in his garden or the deer that wandered near his barn. As we stared at the sky and mountains turning gold through our Dickel, his words drifted out in the air among the cottonwood seeds, which always seemed to be there in warm weather, as if his ranch were suspended in one of those shakeup water balls.

By dark, fishing was usually somewhere on another planet, and I would wind up driving the mountain passes back to Bozeman at two or three in the morning, drunk and depressed. But by midmorning, I would hear again the merry jingle of my telephone, and it would be the Captain. "Let's go fishing tomorrow. Really."

The fishing trips that Richard and I planned in detail but never went on were probably the most interesting. Because of his fascination with small streams, he always liked the creeks in Bozeman city limits. One of them, Sourdough Creek, runs right under the Eagles Bar (about two blocks from my house), where he spent most of his drinking time here. Once, while we were walking from the Eagles to my house, we saw a little girl pull a brook trout that weighed almost a pound out from under a tire store. That really got him going. He wondered how fishing was under the Eagles Bar, under Main Street or in Bogart Park next to my house. The only obstacle in our way to finding out was a law restricting fishing within the city limits to children under the age of twelve.

Later, over Dickel in the Eagles, our plan began to take shape. We would make plywood cutouts of barefoot boys with straw hats and weeds in their teeth and hide behind them while we fished. We were so proud of our plan that we decided we should bring a photographer along and publish our expedition in some classy magazine like *Gray's Sporting Journal*. Of course, the plan never materialized. Now, I guess, if I'm going to follow through with it, I will have to make plywood cutouts of both a kid and Richard.

The last, and now, under the circumstances, the saddest fishing trip the Captain and I ever planned was to take place in the Bay area in August. Since I still have his letters that set the plan in motion, I'll let Richard tell part of the story. I was teaching summer school at MSU in Bozeman when I got a letter from Richard letting me know he was in Bolinas:

> June 8, 1984
> *Dear Greg,*
> Fooled you! doubled back, returned to America, and I'm out here in my house in Bolinas where I plan on spending the summer before returning to Montana in the fall. There's a lot of work I want to do and I think this is a good place to do it. It's interesting to be back in America, but you knew that all the time, anyway.
> Love,
> Richard

Glad to know he was back and hoping Montana wasn't too far in his future, I wrote him a letter pissing and moaning about my teaching and telling him that I would be playing songs at an anti-gold-mining fundraiser in Nevada City, California, in June. Gary Snyder and the people who were putting it on were paying to fly me down and back to Bozeman, so there was really no way I could visit the Captain. I had to get right back for classes. But anyway, he wrote me the following:

> June 15, 1984
> *Dear Greg,*
> I just got your letter. You poor sack of shit!
> I don't have a telephone and may not get one, but my neighbor does and he'll come over and get me if somebody calls. His number is ——-——-———-. I use his telephone sparingly, so don't spread it all over the landscape of Montana. That's an interesting vision: Greggie wandering all over Montana, spreading ——-——-———- on everything he comes across: dogs, trees, rocks, etc.
> Anyway, O unhappy one, I sure would like to see you. We'll get together for certain when you come down in July. Any chance in June? It's only a few more fucking hours down from Nevada City. I know somebody out here who's got a salmon boat docked a few hundred yards away.
> It's something to think about.
> Let me know.
> Don't be afraid of the telephone number.
> Love,
> Richard

Since I was going to the Bay area to visit my brother in late July and early August, I knew I would be seeing Richard, so I decided to get feisty. I knew his M.O. He was just trying to lure me over for Dickel drinking. Besides, one of my friends had told me that El Niño had wiped out most of the salmon fishing in the Bay area for a long time. So I wrote him back, saying he'd have to get up awfully early in the morning to fool a wily Oklahoman: I knew that the salmon fishing was shot. I wound up my letter with a hypothetical *Ancient Mariner* story that ended something like, "Niño, Niño, everywhere and all the salmon shrank," and he responded as follows:

June 23, 1984
Dear Greg,
The next time I pull a salmon out of the beautiful cold waters of the Pacific Ocean, I'll say, "This one is for Greggie. A loser in Montana."
Love from the deck,
Richard

After that letter, I made some feeble response, knowing that I was fencing with a master of ridicule and saying that we would solve the salmon question when I came down to visit my brother. Richard's next response was to the point:

July 2, 1984
Dear Loser (formerly known as Greggie):
Dream on . . .
Losers tend to have loser friends.
"She says . . . El Niño . . . changed . . . currents . . . salmon . . . moved . . . out."
That was last year.
It's nice to have good friends, loser.
Excuse me while I have this delightful young girl place another bite of freshly caught salmon in my jaws.
Thank you, dear.
No, we'll do that later again. You can rest for a while, honey.
Now, where was I? O, yes, writing to a loser.
Excuse me again—

No honey, I don't have losers for friends, this one is a
special case. Don't worry your pretty little head about it.
    "She says…El Niño…changed…currents…salmon…
moved out … "
    Yes, yes, yes.
    Meester Keeler. Why not do you geet me a salmon?!!!
    [a spot on the paper with an arrow to it and a note]
    (Caused by another bite of salmon being put in my
mouth)
        Love,
        Richard

Of course, when I got to the Bay area, the number Richard had given me didn't exactly work like a charm. I called
the people at the number, and they said they'd leave my message and number for Richard. But somehow, after a week or so
of back-and-forth message leaving, we still hadn't talked. In
the meantime, my car had broken down and was in the most
expensive garage in San Francisco (since they were the only
ones who could find parts for it); my older son, Chris, had
been picked up and released by the Moonies and the salmon
were definitely biting like crazy. I sat down by the Berkeley pier
and watched Japanese tourists come in from charter boats with
huge bags of them.
    Finally, I got through to the Captain, and he said, "Here's the
plan. I have this friend, Bob, in Stinson Beach who has a hot-
rod salmon boat with a couple of great big motors in it. We'll
come down from Bolinas to Fisherman's Wharf in it, pick you
up there, go out and murder salmon, then bring them back to
North Beach and have my friend who owns a Japanese restaurant prepare them especially for us." Of course, as it turned
out, Bob's boat wasn't working right, and the Japanese restaurant owner loaned Richard his .44 magnum.

Why The Bunny Didn't Hold Her Breath

Perhaps because I saw what fishing fame ultimately did to Richard, I inevitably either blew it or didn't follow up whenever angling brought me into a brush with bright lights and the big time. In the early nineties, I fell in with David Behr, a friend across the alley in Bozeman who had ESPN connections. After hiring me to be the warm-up act for a John Prine concert, David decided I was star material and contacted his friend in the television industry, Larry Lindberg, to see if we might tape some segments for ESPN.

We decided on "Mountain Guy" for a working title and prepared to head out for the lower Gallatin to see what we could come up with. Before we left, David said to Judy, "You'd better prepare yourself to be a wealthy woman. Television can be mighty lucrative."

Judy looked at me in my torn and stinking fishing outfit, then back at David and said, "I don't think I'll be holding my breath."

"You just wait and see," said David.

Later, on the river, as I tried to slip a small party hat over the head of a sucker I had just caught, David started to get an inkling of why The Bunny wasn't holding her breath. The script that I had written for our first little vignette went something like this:

Greg reels in pre-caught sucker on fly rod, then faces camera with majestic Montana scenery behind him.

Greg: Here in Montana, we always release our suckers, but
before we do, we reward them for participating in the
angling experience so they will look forward to being
caught again.

*Greg reaches into vest, pulls out miniature paper party hat and
pulls elastic band under sucker's chin.*

Greg: Yes, here in Montana, we give our suckers a little party
before we release them.

*Greg moves sucker up and down rapidly so that it appears
to be having a good time and then pulls a little blowout party
noisemaker from his vest and blows it.*

Greg: Wheeeeeeeee, wheeeeeee, go my little friend, and
remember, every time you get caught, it's not a tragedy, it's
a party.

*Shot of sucker swimming off with party hat sticking up like a
little shark fin.*

For some reason that eludes me to this day, the segment
never aired. In fact, only one of the shows we taped ever aired
on ESPN, and that was *Salmon Fly Guy.* For *Salmon Fly Guy,*
we drove to the Madison River near Ennis, and the annual late
spring *Pterernarchis Californica* (salmon fly) hatch. Once we
got there, we had to decide what we were going to DO with
the salmon flies to make an interesting show, so we went into a
local fly shop and found a brochure on the insect's life cycle.

Over a burger at lunch in a café, I did my best to memorize
the stages of the cycle so that I would sound like an expert on
the subject; then we drove back to the river and started taping.
To lend some action to the narration, David got on his hands
and knees out of camera range and released the giant insects
onto the legs of my pants so that, when they followed their
instinct to climb upward, they would crawl over my neck,
beard, face and hat while I was talking.

The shot was working like a charm. I expertly chatted away
with the huge flies teetering on my mustache and eyebrows.

"Yes," I said, "me and my buddies [crawl, crawl] the salmon flies [teeter, teeter] know how to appreciate a late spring day."

But then a crusty-looking old fisherman popped his head out from the door of an adjacent pickup camper and said, "That's 'I,' not 'me.'"

"Cut, cut," said Larry.

"What the hell," said David.

"That's 'I,' not 'me,'" said Crusty. "I'm a high school English teacher and I know about these things. You're using the objective case when you should be using the nominative."

I wanted to say, "Pardon me, Mr. Fuck, but you just ruined a fucking shot we've been setting up for fucking hours. I fucking know what fucking case I'm using. I'm a fucking English profuckingfessor. I'm just trying to sound fucking folksy, O-fucking K?"

But instead, I said, "Good point," and we returned to taping —after David had recaptured all the salmon flies and put them on my legs again so that they would recommence their trek toward my head.

That video aired on New Year's Eve of 1991. What little pay I got for it probably came out of Larry's own pocket.

"Rich, I tell you, rich!" said The Bunny.

A couple of summers before the salmon fly debacle, I was sitting high on a stage prop holding a fly rod, with Jeff and Beau Bridges battling at the end of my line. This time, the brush was with fame instead of fortune, but the effect was much the same.

I had come to be sitting on this stage prop through a circuitous sequence of events that commenced when my friend Michael Devine decided to host a biweekly extravaganza in Livingston, Montana, called *The Main Street Show*—and he asked me to be his sidekick. Besides local and regional acts, Michael would sometimes book the more famous friends he had made while designing and building houses in the area.

Occasionally Jeff Bridges would show up to play a song or two, and once, Peter Fonda wore some wild optometrist's glasses while Larry Hagman held a small battery-powered fan in his face; then some guy shuffled a big black bear onto the tiny stage.

But this particular show, entitled "The Woolly Worm Weview" after one of the area's more popular wet flies, was even more extravagant. Instead of indoors on the stage of the Danforth Art Gallery on Main Street, this show was outside on the stage of the amphitheater in Sacajawea Park on the Yellowstone River. The mood of the event was set when, during the opening scenes, a duck flew into some power wires, temporarily shorting out the stage lights and the Coke machine. The cast of characters included Michael Devine as Zeus, The Bunny as Hera, Vanessa Brittan as the River Goddess, John Stillman as the Woolly Worm and me as the fisherman. Michael told me that he had found a couple of friends to play the River Gods who would battle to determine whether or not I lost the Woolly Worm when I snagged it on the bottom of the river, but I had no idea that it would be the Bridges brothers.

As I was waiting backstage for my climactic scene and Jeff and Beau showed up and engaged me in a last-minute rehearsal, I didn't have time to be nervous or impressed. They were very serious, and though they had no speaking lines, they wanted to know who should dash where and when and who should grab whom and how. After Michael gave them some brief directions, I assumed my perch on a tall plywood structure and cast my line to the stage, while the Bridgeses donned odd masks and rushed onstage beneath me. The ensuing battle was so vigorous and intense I feared that one of the brothers had injured the other, but when the show was over, they vanished as mysteriously as they had appeared.

Part IV

… and nobody, nobody knows what's
going to happen to anybody, besides
the forlorn rags of growing old. …

Sal in Jack Kerouac's *On the Road*

Some Town Trout

In the late winter of 1993, my friend David McCumber, who was a founding editor of *Big Sky Journal*, asked me to start writing a column for the magazine in conjunction with the artist Parks Reese. How could I have known that this first column, published in the premier issue in the spring of 1994, would be a death knell for innocence and security and would portend the years of betrayal and chaos that followed?

On evenings when the spring thaw is going full blast, I like to sleep with the bedroom window open. Though I live just two blocks off Bozeman's Main Street, I can hear Sourdough Creek swollen and roaring down from the Hyalites where elk are dipping for a drink, down through hayfields, then subdivisions, then the older tree-lined streets like my own, then under the heart of the town, then out to join the East Gallatin, the Gallatin, the Missouri, the Mississippi and the Gulf. Drifting off to that sound, I seldom remember my dreams, but my waking thoughts are as diverse as the way light hits the water when I watch from a bridge half a block from my house.

Figuratively, my friends and family have been woven into that sound over the past eighteen years, and literally the beautiful brook, cutthroat and rainbow trout have occupied the stream's small wilderness as it mocks the brief civilization through which it passes. When I first moved here, I was barbaric enough to try to catch them. I skulked through the backyards of condos and four-plexes, an Okie astounded that such pristine water could keep its cool in the middle of town, my fly rod held low so as not to be seen from picture windows.

Dangling an Adams, a Trude or a Joe's Hopper as the season required, I caught amazingly fat and bright trout that took my fly without question. As these porcine brookies flashed down the delicate riffles and behind the undercut banks, I knew I hadn't lived a decent enough life to deserve a place like this.

And it was true. I was totally out of bounds. One evening a kind but panicked woman came striding across her backyard to inform me that I had just caught Helen, a trout whom she had befriended to the point that it would dart to a certain part of the pool to be fed Green Giant corn niblets. Dejected and ashamed, I released Helen while the woman warned me that only children under twelve could legally fish within Bozeman's city limits.

It wasn't until a few years later, when my younger son was old enough to use a rod, that I dared to pursue these trout again, guiding him and his friend down the grassy paths next to the stream, but even then, to be legal, my fishing thrills had to be vicarious, and soon the boys realized that they weren't so much experiencing quality time as being used as an excuse for a pathetic adult to act out his streamside fantasies. Besides, they were just flirting with the stream and they wanted to have their way with it—like my older son, who had donned cutoffs, hopped on an inner tube and floated its mysterious tunnel under Main Street.

Several years after that, Richard Brautigan, who was teaching in my department at the university, suggested that we paint plywood cutouts of young boys wearing straw hats and holding weeds in their teeth and hide behind them while we fished. But, as usual, we wound up sitting in the Eagles Bar and drinking George Dickel instead. In a way, this wasn't too far from the original plan because Sourdough Creek plunges under Main Street just a few feet west of the bar. In the spring, when the place is almost empty and the jukebox isn't going, you can hear it.

That sound holds more now than it did then, and at night when I'm lying in bed, it almost carries too much. My sons and their friends have grown up; Richard shot himself a decade ago; two girls drowned under the Eagles after a night on the town. The fish are still beautiful but not so much fun any more. Even the caddis fly hatches seem a bit dazed and confused when I stand in the front yard and watch them in the evening. Across the way, Earl, the retired county surveyor, surveys them with me while they dance over the street as if it were water.

Chances are, they're not confused at all. Behind my house, the alley is strewn with rocks from the old streambed where it probably flowed a thousand years ago, and I'm sure the relatives of those flies have danced for millennia back and forth over the valley where geology and weather chose to move the party, the cutthroat trout leaping up through the dance in their own sweet time. These street flies are obviously playing a trick on me and Earl, dancing a few centuries out of place.

Or maybe we're just learning to read. Perhaps trout, bugs and moving water are print in the book of our place. Downstream, where Sourdough runs a few feet from the public library, my wife spends much of her time reading books and water, glancing down and then out the window, confusing words with the light and sound that inspire them, and when I think of this, all the loss and transience seem only natural. Soon Sourdough will be clear enough for fishing, but I won't attempt it any more. Instead, I'll catch grasshoppers and drop them from various bridges while I walk upstream toward work. Perhaps I'll look silly to passing bikers and joggers as I hunch and pounce in the grass, my sport coat hung on a branch above my briefcase; but if they're foolish enough to question me, I'll give them a brief reading lesson and make them watch a grasshopper drift until a delicate nose breaks the surface.

Pity and Terror
in Sun Valley

James Dickey's poem "Adultery" says that guilt is magical, which I now believe to be the case, though magic has at least as much to do with people getting burned at the stake as it does with Tinkerbell. It was the early spring of 1994, and I had just met someone with whom I knew I was bound to become adulterous. I was so blinded by this knowledge that, as I drove from Bozeman toward Ketchum–Sun Valley to perform my songs for what my contract described as a "group of movie moguls," I stopped near Rexburg, Idaho, and bought a pair of amber-tinted sunglasses.

I only remember a few images from that trip, but they remain vivid. The prevailing image was the sensation of being literally pulled in two directions at once, as if my car and body wanted to go forward and into the future and my heart and mind wanted to go home to Judy. This sensation was to persist until the second millennium. Next was the imagery of the performance itself. I know very little about Hollywood, but the person in charge of my appearance was Frank Wells, at the time Disney's second in command. He was a kind, well-spoken man who warned me before I played that the comedian they had hired for this function the previous year had bombed because he had ridiculed the audience. Since I hadn't planned on ridiculing anyone, I figured I was safe.

I was also informed before I played that the moguls before me included a Zanuck and Barbra Streisand's producer/

hairdresser. That still didn't faze me since I only had a vague sense of who those people were, but as I perched myself on a stool before the group, I did notice that Clint Eastwood was sitting at the table directly in front of me, and as I played my songs, it seemed that everyone was looking at him to see whether they should respond or not. For the first few songs, Clint wasn't laughing, so neither was anyone else. But when I played a song about the horror of babies showing up on airplanes, at restaurants and in movie theaters, Clint doubled over laughing, and so did everyone else. Later, I found out that, at sixty, he had just had a baby with his twenty-something wife, and he and everyone else thought that I was specifically making fun of him. Of course, in my mind, I was only aware that I was bound for adultery with a twenty-something woman, and I wanted to go home to Judy.

At the end of the performance, Frank Wells doubled my fee and told me that this was an annual event and he wanted me to come back every year. I was on a double high driving home because (1) I was going home to Judy and (2) I was having fantasies of a glitzy future, replete with movie stars and a young blonde. While my mind was being torn in these two directions, I looked out my car window and noticed that I was driving past the meadow where I had rolled in sagebrush so that I might smell manly and like the Great Out of Doors before I visited Muffet Hemingway twenty-two years earlier. I slowed down and contemplated doing the same thing again, mostly out of sheer confusion, when I saw some young calves gamboling across the same meadow. I thought that one of the calves was gamboling with particular abandon until I realized that it was hurling itself along because its two front legs were mutated into withered little sticks. Then I remembered that I was near Arco, Idaho, basically a nuclear waste dump.

It wasn't until a week later that I got a letter from Frank

Wells's secretary, saying that he had died when his helicopter crashed near Sun Valley while he and his group were skiing a couple of days after my performance and that it was only by a fluke that Clint Eastwood hadn't died in that helicopter too.

Not Fishing:
Greg and Dick's
Not-So-Excellent
Adventure

. . . .

"Go ahead," said Dick, "you're not getting any younger; in fact, you're quite a bit closer to your death than you are to your birth."

It was the spring of 1994, and Dick had been talking to Greg for several years now, ever since Judy had come down with an incurable bladder disease that would keep her in deep pain for much of her remaining life. When Dick talked to Greg, it was not at all like the tree that talked to Judy and suggested that she might make a good candidate for the Queen of Dondore. No, Dick was just trying to get Greg to arrange his life around the needs of, well, Dick, and recently another woman had been making herself available.

"But I said 'in sickness and in health,'" said Greg.

"Get real," said Dick. "You said it to a duck-hunting J.P. in Elko, Nevada."

"No," said Greg, "I said it to Judy."

"Listen," said Dick, "you're a man. You have a man's needs. It's only natural."

Greg hadn't figured out yet that when Dick said *you* he really meant *me*. Having been born in 1946, Dick was at the head of the Me Generation.

"Surely," said Dick, "you can arrange things so that every-body's happy—so that you can stick with The Bunny and I get HER." Dick was pointing at a young woman sitting in his office at the university.

And so it came to pass that Greg started lying, and worst of all, he was lying to The Bunny, and next to worst of all, he was lying about fishing; for instead of his passion, it became an excuse, a smokescreen behind which he fulfilled the wishes of Dick.

This arrangement, of course, took a huge toll on Greg's conscience, so while Dick lived in temporary bliss, Greg lived in permanent fear. When Greg said to The Bunny, "I'm going fishing. I'll be back in a few hours," he knew that he was really saying, "I'm going to please Dick by making a mockery of my two religions, monogamy and fishing. I'll be back in a few hours."

Of course, the young woman also got her fair share of this deception, for when Dick was with her, he had to pretend that Greg was there too—and not off in a corner saying, "Oh my god, what have I done." And because she was witness to Greg's deceptions concerning Judy, it was much easier for her to see through Dick's thin veneer of sweet talk, and soon she began to tire of the situation.

And Greg began to tire of his guilty conscience, so he spilled the beans to The Bunny, who was, of course, terrified because she had always considered Greg to be her rock, especially when she was facing a life of chronic pain and drudge work as a com-position instructor, so she implored Greg not to leave her.

But it was too late for Greg. Dick had him by the soul. Greg tried all sorts of things to get his soul back. He would, for example, go fishing, but since he had tarnished fishing by using it as an excuse for Dick, it just became an extension of his guilt. Greg even went to the extreme of becoming a wilderness ranger for two summers, clomping hundreds of miles through the Lee Metcalf Wilderness as an assistant to Jon Anderson, his former student who was a full-time wilderness ranger.

It would seem that trudging for days on end through the wilderness might have helped Greg to get his soul back, but out of physical necessity, Greg was compelled to drag Dick along with him. In these situations, Dick always felt that he had better things to do. Poor Jon Anderson had to listen to Greg argue with Dick. Over hill and dale, through some of the most breathtaking landscapes in America, Greg would go on and on, and Jon would occasionally go "Hmmm," or "It seems to me that you're saying . . ." Jon should have been getting a hundred dollars an hour instead of ten, because he was not only serving as a wilderness ranger; he was also serving as a therapist.

And what was Judy doing while Greg was off clomping and clomping, sporadically coming down from the mountains to accommodate Dick's whims? She was walking in little circles around the coffee table in the living room of the tiny house where they had raised two boys who had now left for their own lives, wearing a path with her pain and terror. She was no longer anybody's Bunny. She was in too much pain to be the Queen of Dondore. She wanted to die.

The Sea Widow

So what did Greg do when he realized the depths of Judy's despair? Did he rush to her side to comfort her? Did he accompany her to marriage counselors? Did he drink and smoke and drink and smoke? Did he start taking prescribed medications? Yes, he did all of the above, but Dick still had him by the soul, so he divorced her.

Greg, however, found that the legality of the divorce was as flimsy to him as that of the marriage had been to Dick. While Judy was struggling to stay alive for reasons that became less and less apparent to her, Greg wandered in a no-man's-land somewhere between his heart and his crotch. One day, as he was driving to a trailhead in the Spanish Peaks to meet up with Jon Anderson for a four-day hitch, he passed the cabin where his baby son Max had gone "womp" and run to the arms of the Queen of Dondore. Actually, it wasn't a cabin any more. It was just a bare spot, for the cabin had burned down many years before.

It was then that he started writing some poems in his head. The poems were from the perspective of a woman who lived on a stormy island in Great Britain's North Sea. He didn't know how this woman got into his mind, but he thought of her as the Sea Widow because her husband had been a fisherman and he had drowned in the Atlantic. This is the poem that came to him when he passed the burned cabin.

Her Prayer

God who doesn't
exist in the black sky
where the wind never stops,

bring him back,
and I promise to be as
flat and stupid as you

who lets the gulls
gawk and hack
carrion on wet rocks.

God who would allow
the sea to suck his flesh
to pale shreds if

stars weren't cold bits
of nothing in my hideous winter,
choke on your spit

like the waves that won't
stop their blather against
my sagging walls.

God who is nothing but
hate in my gullet,
at least give me his

bones, and I'll sit
on your dumb-show pews
till I die or go blind.

Double or Nothing

. . . .

For another year, Greg wandered in his no-man's-land, trying to get his soul back. Some of the time he spent in the Owl Bar in Livingston, Montana, drinking fishbowls of vodka. He even rented a small house in that town in an effort to find some peace of mind, but one day while he was grading papers in the house, a Vietnam veteran blew his brains out in the little park across the street. After the fire department had hosed away most of the blood, Greg went into his front yard and found a piece of skull the size and shape of a silver dollar. Shortly after that he moved out of the house and tried to go back to Judy, but his dick wouldn't let him, so he rented a room at the Murray Hotel in Livingston.

Greg went to several therapists, who told him that he needed to make peace with his inner child. He figured that they were actually referring to his dick, but they didn't want to call it that. One therapist would have him sit in a chair facing an empty chair and tell him to pretend that his inner child was sitting there so that he could ask his inner child questions.

And then she would have him sit in the empty chair and be his inner child asking his older self questions.

None of this worked very well for Greg because, to him, he was still just talking to his dick.

On his many visits to the Owl Bar, between fishbowls of vodka, Greg had become acquainted with another young woman, and his dick, of course, wanted to hog the show. This time, however, his dick would almost get him killed, for the woman was being stalked by a fisherman who wrote books about fishing, a fisherman who had lost his obsession for fishing and had become obsessed with her. This man's dick had won over the rest of him so entirely that nothing of the world existed but itself and the young woman. If Greg ever had a double, this man was it.

Greg went to court to help the woman get a restraining order against the man, but the order only intensified his obsession. One night when Greg was at Judy's house trying to comfort her because of a particularly severe attack of her bladder disease, the phone rang, and it was this man. He wanted Greg to come to a Bozeman restaurant so that they could talk. So, a few minutes later, leaning across the table in their booth, the man told him of how he had tried to poison him, how he had broken into his room at the Murray Hotel and removed a pill from a prescription of hydrocodone for Greg's wife, a prescription that Greg had borrowed because he had just had a tooth pulled. The man told him how he had drilled out the tablet and filled it with sodium cyanide, which he had stolen from the chemistry lab at the university in Bozeman, and how he had then returned the pill to the prescription bottle in his room.

He told Greg how, a day later, he had second thoughts and broke back into his room and removed the pill. Greg knew that much of what the man said must have been true because he had identified the prescription so accurately, and the only reason Greg had not taken the pill was that he never felt any pain after the tooth was pulled. He also knew that if the man had left the pill in the bottle, he would have brought it to Judy's house, and she would have taken it because her pain had not stopped for a month.

That next week, the man broke his neck and died when his dick made him drive off of a bridge over a railroad track between Belgrade and Manhattan, Montana. He was fleeing police officers, who had pursued him because his dick had made him violate the restraining order and try to break into the young woman's house. It was then that Greg decided, come hell or high water, to put a damper on his dick.

Whirling

The River is as far as I can move
from the world of numbers:
I'm all for retreats, escapes,
a 47 yr. old runaway.

Jim Harrison

. . . .

In the spring of 1995, a universe away from the previous year,
when I wrote "Some Town Trout," I published this column in
Big Sky Journal on the human implications of whirling disease,
which was running rampant in rainbow trout at the time. It
still has some truth to it, both about whirling and about my
efforts to, as Gary Snyder had instructed me years before, stay
in place.

This spring, a bunch of rainbow trout on the lower Madison
are suffering from whirling disease. I've never seen this virus in
action, but I'd guess it makes the trout emulate those Turkish
dervishes who go into a trance and spin in circles while tortur-
ing themselves. Apparently the disease travels downstream
in tiny spores and upstream in big trout, and there's hardly
any stopping it. The big old angelfish in my aquarium had
the disease too. He whirled for a good four months, then did
a postmortem whirl down the toilet. The virus must travel
through air and glass; I think it's even infected me.

I was lummoxing through the Gallatin in my Neoprenes the
other day, and noticed that I was wading in deep, fast March
water where I was likely to die. I looked upstream to my fishing
partner, Jack Jelinski, who had waded these rapids before, and
he made a little circular motion with his index finger. His gesture

hinted at several options: (1). Crazy. (2). Whoop-de-do, big
stud thinks he can wade four-foot rapids. (3). Only an idiot
in his midlife crisis would stand in water like that. (4). Go
forward. No, go back. No, go forward.

A man of action, I followed number four, bouncing and
spinning in a circle from boulder to boulder, wondering where
the shallow water started. Later, after I had whirled my way to
the bank, Jack said that I looked real funny—out there spinning like that. Here is approximately what he was trying to
convey with his gesture: "You're standing in the spot where
I started whirling when I stood there. Damn scary, isn't it."
A ray of hope hit me then and there. He had made it into his
fifties—alive.

Occasionally, things tend to whirl in a river: trout, bark,
people, bugs, bubbles. Maybe that's why I try to walk through
one as often as possible—to understand things like gravity,
direction, depth, riffles, eddies, pools and runs, and that sometimes point A to point B isn't a straight line. The poor rainbows
and their disease, and maybe this ditzy prose, are the downside
of this progression. The upside? Obviously, the water ouzel.

These birds know streams better than anyone else above
the water line, and they don't whirl. They dip. Perhaps you've
seen them doing their little knee bends next to some fast water.
Sometimes when I'm not floundering through rapids, I stop
and watch them, and after years of investigation, I've decided
that they dip to account for refraction, so they can figure the
proper angle of light and see a bug out there at the bottom of
the fastest current. I used to pity them as they plunged into the
torrent and popped out on a rock. I imagined them struggling
in horror across the bottom of a fast stream, risking their lives
for lunch every day. It was only after the first dozen or so years
of observation that my pity turned to envy, when I realized
their lives are actually sort of casual. I finally saw one clearly
and realized that it wasn't whirling, struggling and grasping

its way across the bottom. No, it was just kind of wandering around down there with a bemused disinterest—a bit like a robin looking for worms on a courthouse lawn or an aging bachelor pushing a shopping cart through Safeway.

I try to imagine the ouzel's reaction to an infected rainbow trout helicoptering past its rock, or a large white guy exploring the possibilities of Anglo-Saxon expletives as he careens into water over his waders, but such phenomena probably do not register on the ouzel's delicate instruments, unless perhaps they block its view of a bug.

The ouzel has obviously learned how to live in a river. I'd like to do that too, but when I try to look down into the water—even when I do a few deep knee bends—I generally see only the reflections of trees and clouds swirling into each other. If I knew my life like an ouzel knows a river, instead of longing for rehearsals, I might wander in and out of surfaces and alien environments, at home with water, air and earth. Love would be as easy as diving off a rock, and death would be as familiar as the moon seen from underwater. Yes, in ouzel mode, I might shoulder the pain and wreckage I've inflicted on myself and those I love as an ouzel shoulders the current—not so much as a burden but as a way of staying in place where everything else is moving. My left brain could become my ouzel brain, and I could pursue every illusion my other lobe sprang on me with no fear of being sucked beneath a rock ledge or swept over the nearest cataract. And at dusk, I could dodge down to the river through the high pines and slightly bend my knees in the presence of my goofy little ouzel god—no big splashy divinity, just a bird that knows how to handle rivers.

But alas, I'm no ouzel, and I'm whirling again—a bit like the poor schmuck I saw on the Yellowstone last spring. His guide had left the McKenzie boat to retrieve an oar and the boat had drifted away, bobbing in crazy circles downstream toward Livingston as the panicked client rowed furiously at his one oar. At the time, I was wondering where he thought he was going, but any more, it doesn't seem to make much difference. Whether from a missing oar, a virus, a crisis or a friend's gesture, we whirlers are at the river's mercy, and the river has its own plans.

Too Many Bunnies

And what of me, the vestigial remnant of Greg's fishing-self? There was a little more to this story than I've let on. After all, I was both Greg and Dick—and still am for that matter. While they duked it out over relationships, I was drumming my fingers on various countertops and bars or lolling and yawning on the logs and rock outcroppings of the Lee Metcalf Wilderness, waiting to get back to the fish. Now, looking back through what Faulkner called the bottleneck of the most recent decade, I wish that I'd been a little more patient with everyone involved. Greg and Dick were actually pretty boring compared to Bunny Girl, Jon Anderson, the Bull-Waif—and especially Judy.

Bunny Girl was the young woman sitting in my office at the beginning of the saga. She was twenty years my junior and looked like a cross between the model Claudia Schiffer and Roger Rabbit's heartthrob, Jessica. Green eyes, blonde hair, miniskirt and cowboy boots aside, I was a goner when she pointed to her front teeth and said, "When I was a kid, they called me Bunny Girl." And she was a tormented artist to boot. Before I quite realized what was happening, I wandered into her first major exhibit, a series of chainsaw sculptures blending pre-Colombian figures with embodiments of her own history. The most striking one, the one that made me start questioning my sanity, was a totem pole. At the bottom was a fish-like Mayan deity with a beheading axe, and above that was a horrified bunny girl, then above her, a woman putting a severed head in a sacrificial basin at the top of the pole. To me, the head looked strikingly like my own.

A fish-person chasing a bunny-person struggling behind a woman with my head in tow? I was pretty sure I'd had that dream.

Not only was the Bunny Girl a student and tormented artist, but during the summers, she was a wilderness ranger, and before long, unable to distinguish my dick from a totem pole, I was making feverish plans to accompany her as an official ranger's assistant, and, hounded by my aforementioned guilt and deceit and blocking the fact that Judy wasn't part of this phantasmagoric dreamscape, I not only spilled the beans to her; I told her that I was going to spend the summer in the Montana wilderness with Bunny Girl. Yes, from that nebulous DMZ between dream and reality, I told her this like a boy might tell his mother that he was going to spend the summer at Bible camp with a friend.

I have recounted this next scene to a therapist while she moved a pencil's eraser back and forth in front of my eyes in an attempt to distract me and short-circuit the trauma of the memory: Judy is crying and suicidal in her physical and emotional pain, begging me not to go and hanging on to me by my T-shirt, but I literally tear myself away from her.

With the horror of this image fresh in my mind, I left our little house and our long marriage, drove a bleary-eyed eighty miles to a trailhead, walked eight miles up into the Taylor-Hilgard Wilderness and collapsed on the trail in my sleeping bag at around midnight, a mile short of the lake where Bunny Girl had told me she would be camping.

When I found her the next morning, she was also traumatized because a bear had been sniffing and poking around her tent in the night. Before she had gone to sleep, she had dabbed Tiger Balm on her temples to salve a raging headache, forgetting that she was simultaneously dabbing her temples with bear attractant. Earlier that day she had found another surefire bear attractant—a dead packhorse that had fallen and eviscerated itself on a snag near the lake above her camp. She told me I was lucky that I hadn't gotten a visit from Smokey too, since I had slept on the trail with jerky and granola next to me in my backpack. Later, she reported the carcass to Forest Service headquarters, and subsequently they sent in a team with dynamite and blew what remained of it to smithereens, but not before Bunny Girl and I had both unwittingly done our best to serve ourselves up to grizzly bears as side dishes to a dead packhorse.

Our first act as ranger and assistant that morning was to practice using her bear spray. She read the instructions on the can as I held it out in front of us and prepared to pull the trigger. Fortunately, she could read faster than I could pull, because I had the nozzle pointed at our faces.

I might have somehow been able to remain rational about Bunny Girl and her realm of dreams, give her my love, wish her all the luck in the world and return to my tried-and-true Bunny had she not, in a moment of reckless abandon, whispered these six words: "I want to have your baby." So what if our pairing was equivalent, in fish terminology, to the mating of a brook trout and a coelacanth? So what if I'd had a vasectomy twenty years before? So what if that vasectomy was at about the same time that Christopher had won the second-grade Halloween contest with a Frankenstein costume I made for him? So what if Bunny Girl, who remembered wishing that her own father had cared enough about her to make her such a costume, was in that same class.

Against all my vows, my monogamous instincts and my true heart, I divorced Judy and moved over the pass from Bozeman to Livingston in hopes of joining Bunny Girl in the realm of dreams. But when she started to get a snoot-full of the terror and confusion that accompany two people who still love each other but are trying to separate after twenty years of marriage, she fled to a cabin near a mountaintop in Paradise Valley and has pretty much stayed there, occasionally descending to commit blatant acts of life imitating art. For example, a few years ago I saw in the local paper that a candy company had flown her to Wisconsin to sculpt a giant Easter bunny out of chocolate.

Walking Small

A few pages ago, when I labeled this chaotic stage "Not Fishing," I wasn't being entirely honest—but what else is new. Jon Anderson took me fishing. Jon Anderson took me many places other than death, which is where I wanted to go during much of that bottomless summer. Jon had been a student in several of my classes and was good at writing poetry and post-structural criticism. Both of these talents surprised me since his casual conversation contained a few of the grammatical glitches common to small-town Montana, where he grew up.

One afternoon I was sitting on the lawn of the local cultural center, listening to a rock band and staring hollow-eyed into that limbo where I could neither, in good conscience, spend the summer with Bunny Girl nor return to Judy, when Jon plopped down beside me.

"Do you still want be a ranger this summer?" said Jon.

"What do you mean, still?" I said. "How did you know I wanted to be one in the first place?"

"These things get around," said Jon as his glass eye wandered off toward the band and his good eye stared straight into both of mine. "I might not be as pretty as she is, but I've rangered for quite a bit longer, and if you decide to join me, we won't be bivouacking next to a gutted packhorse or trying to mace ourselves in the face."

I didn't even ask how details of my clandestine wilderness rendezvous with Bunny Girl had made headlines in Forest Service gossip.

"Sure," I said, "why not?"

So for the next two summers, the young protégé took the

old mentor under his wing and showed him how to be a wilderness ranger—a designation that might sound epic and heroic, but in its details is as humdrum and practical as any government job. Basically, we inventoried campsites by tallying up the damage campers had inflicted; then we did our best to repair the damage and make the site look pristine so the next campers to come through would have a true "wilderness experience" before they messed it up again. While wheezing along behind John for a few hundred miles and trying to stave off the conflicting desires to (1) go join Bunny Girl in her adjacent wilderness because she was alone now (save for a loop or two with a gimped-up ex, a bored administrator from headquarters and a landowner from property bordering the Taylor-Hilgard Wilderness who came crashing through the deadfall to propose) or (2) flee to Bozeman and the arms of my angry and devastated but tried-and-true Bunny, I composed the following song with pennywhistles and a passionate Irish melody running through my head.

Wilderness Ranger

Well, you're up in the mornin' and out clearin' trail
To facilitate camping convenience.
You put on your pickle shirt, tuck in your tail.
Your hat says USFS Genius.
You carry a shovel and bury your waste.
Use your stove to avoid fire danger.
And camp at least 200 feet from the lake.
It's the code of the Wilderness Ranger.

And you know that your job will be doin' some good
When you do a campsite inventory.
You broadcast the ashes and old firewood
To rehab its wilderness glory.
Yes, it's bust up the fire rings and count damaged trees.

Make it look like no one ever came here,
While you're dodgin' the horse-flies, mosquitoes and
bees.
It's the life of a Wilderness Ranger.

Well, it's gorp for your breakfast and gorp for your lunch.
For your dinner it's freeze-dried refritos.
For a snack, bring some sun-dried papayas to munch,
And an energy bar and some Cheetos.
You pick up the pieces of melted tinfoil.
Make it look like no one ever came here.
Be sure that your water is filtered or boiled.
It's the code of the Wilderness Ranger.

Well, you hike till your feet are all blistered and sore,
Then you hike till there's blisters on blisters.
Don't stop to ask what you are doin' it for,
My wilderness brothers and sisters.
Just hang all your food from the limb of a tree
To minimize campsite bear danger.
With bites on your elbows and scabs on your knees,
You're a certified Wilderness Ranger.

Don't shortcut the switchbacks. Use leaves when you
wipe.
Low impact's the rule from headquarters.
Keep wilderness pristine, at least till you sight
The clear-cuts that lie at the borders.

Jon was always happy to hear me making up songs and
would frequently join me because anything was better than
listening to me vacillate like a tangled wind chime.

Not that we didn't have plenty of other distractions. Sometimes we would encounter hikers on the trail, and they would
give us funny looks because Jon was such an obvious ranger,

what with his clean uniform and soft-spoken manners, and I looked like a such derelict, what with my lack of a uniform, my sweat-stained bandana and my desperate red eyes peering out from under the bill of my filthy cap. John would chat them up for a while, giving them the usual rundown on rules for camping, fishing, shooting and trail use; then he would casually gesture toward me and say, "Gorgo here's on work-release from the prison up at Deer Lodge. Don't pay him no mind. He might be big, but he generally doesn't go for folks unless they look at him funny." Then, while they were trying not to look at me funny, he'd say, "It was a little hard to get him trained, but now he's as good as a mule. Gorgo, get," and he would point to a small boulder in the trail, whereupon I would heft it up grunting and carry it to the side.

Though we were in the Montana wilderness, horses irritated both of us, mainly because, no matter how far we trekked into the heart of the wild, the trails remained horse sewers: columbine glades with crystal springs trickling into horse sewers, dazzling hillsides of Indian paintbrush sloping down to horse sewers, lupine meadows with trout streams meandering beside horse sewers. On occasion, we would encounter riders who would view us scornfully from the shade of their broad-brimmed hats and their high perches of creaking leather while we navigated their sewers on foot. Sometimes they would even stop to engage Jon in conversation.

"Mornin', boys. You two part of a trail crew?"

"No, we're rangers."

"Rangers? In Texas where we come from, you don't see no ranger that don't have him a horse—haw, haw."

"I appreciate your input, pard, but some of us rangers here in Montana get up off our fat asses and walk. It makes for a lot less horseshit."

I never came across Ted Turner, whose ranch borders the Lee Metcalf Wilderness, but Jon encountered him on the paved

road near the trailhead to the Spanish Lakes. Because Jon is a
Christian in the best sense of the word, he found the following
exchange particularly memorable.

"You with the Goddamned Forest Service?"

"Yes, sir."

"I thought I told you son-of-a-bitches to get rid of this Goddamned cattle guard."

"The roads aren't my job, sir, but I'll pass your request on
to headquarters."

"If your Goddamned job doesn't have anything to do with
the Goddamned cattle guard, what is your Goddamned job if
you don't mind my Goddamned asking?"

"I'm a wilderness ranger, sir."

"Well, I'll be Goddamned."

"Yes, sir."

Animals (besides horses) also provided us with some interesting distractions as we walked and camped along the horse
sewers. Perhaps the least among them was Buford Fuzzy, a deer
mouse. We named him that because he reminded us of Buford
Pusser in *Walking Tall*. We thought that Buford should star in
his own movie, *Walking Small*, because he was so brazen in the
way he'd storm into the middle of our camp and take anything
he could carry—like whole Snickers bars.

We also met up with several thousand voles near the top of a
hill that bordered the Turner ranch. Jon started a tradition when
he put on a work glove, sought out the fattest vole, and started
gently poking it in the abdomen with his index finger so that
it rolled over on its back and tried to bite through the glove.

"Pokey, pokey," said Jon to the vole in a Mickey Mouse fal-
setto. This somehow struck a chord with me, and I sought
out my own vole to poke as a sort of last-ditch effort to give
meaning to our job—and my life. What must we have looked
like—two large mammals, grown men, one in uniform, on our
knees making this noise, doing this thing?

Two voles—pokey, pokey.
One treed grouse—pokey, pokey.
One cornered brook trout—pokey, pokey.
One sleeping tiger moth—pokey, pokey.
With the bear and the moose, we decided to keep the pokey
thing figurative.

And there was the fishing, unlike any I had experienced before,
not because it was in the glacial lakes and alpine streams of
the Spanish Peaks and not because of the magic in names like
Chiquita, Champagne, Grayling, Hell Roaring, Big Brother,
Spanish and Diamond. It wasn't even the size and purity of
the fish themselves, not their flesh, pink and gemlike, tasting
of air, pine and glacial melt.

It was Jon. Without him I would have been too numbed and
detached, too caught up in my own psycho-blather, to give
myself over to these things and forget how I'd tarnished this
religion. Who else would have had the tolerance and patience
to play father to my sulking inner child and cajole him into
fishing again?

"Here, Gorgo, take this rod."

"Why?"

"Just take it."

"You rigged it up for me."

"Yes, now cast."

"If you say so."

"See, that's not so bad now, is it?"

"I guess not."

And for a while, I got to be a kid again, running up and
down the banks, screeching and holding up big shiny cutthroat trout for Jon's approval. I became so blinded by my
new lease on fishing at Champagne Lake that I plunged head-
first into a boulder field while carrying a basin of trout fillets
from the pool where I'd cleaned them back to our campsite.

I stumbled into camp, semiconscious and bleeding from my head like a stuck pig, and John picked all two hundred and ten pounds of me up and carried me down to the lake, where he cleaned my wounds, checked my eyes for a concussion, put gauze on my forehead and wrapped that in a bandana.

"Why did you do that?" said Jon.

"I was bringing the fillets back to camp, and I guess I got carried away by their color."

"You mean because they're pink like salmon?

"Pinker."

"Where are they?"

"Over there in that boulder field."

"I'll go get them."

At Diamond Lake, where we had to drop down into a high basin to inventory some campsites, I froze on an outcropping of a perpendicular rock face that dropped twenty feet into steep talus, afraid to climb up or jump down.

"Come on," said Jon, hopping around me like a mountain goat on tiny ledges and footholds.

"I can't."

"But I thought you *wanted* to die."

"I changed my mind."

"Then let's go fishing." With that, he jumped to the talus and glissaded down to the lake, as if his boots were skis and the shale were snow. He made it look so easy that I followed him, relaxing into the fall and slide, down the days and weeks all the way to the end of that high, blue summer.

The Bull-Waif

. . . .

I met the Bull-Waif in Livingston's Owl Bar where I would go with my friend and housemate David McCumber, who was also in the throes of a midlife crisis. I harbored futile hopes either that Bunny Girl would descend from her hilltop fortress and spirit me away to dreamland or that I would lose my fondness for her and return to Judy, free of all my deceit and reckless impulses. As fall gave way to winter, David and I drank successive fishbowls of vodka and entertained the regulars by broadly proclaiming that we had shit ourselves, for, though our pants remained relatively clean, the more profound implications of the phrase weren't much of a stretch. As winter deepened into spring snows, I sank further into depression and isolated myself in a little house next to a park at the south end of Livingston's G Street, only venturing forth to teach my classes over the icy pass in Bozeman during the day and drink during the night. I thought I had reached the bottom when spring arrived, but then a Vietnam vet blew his brains out with a shotgun in the park across the street, and I started drinking during the day.

Some evenings at the Owl, I remained sober enough to barely recognize a small, distinguished-looking local travel and sports writer playing the poker machines with a waif by his side. The way he shepherded her around, I thought that perhaps she was his long-lost daughter or perhaps a sort of Dickensian charge. It wasn't until she showed up to play the poker machines alone one evening that I found it fitting to stroll over and inform her that I had shit myself. In doing so, I recognized her as a student I had known at MSU many years before. Apparently unswayed by my revelation, she continued with her poker machine until it started playing the "Hallelujah Chorus."

"Yes!" she said. "A flush! What was that you were saying? You did something to yourself?"

"Where's your friend?" I said.

"He's *not* my friend."

"OK, where's your, uh, dad?"

"He's *definitely* not that. If you really want to know what he is, I'll tell you. He's a stalker," and as if to illustrate her point, the little man popped in the back door of the bar, saw us, turned red and scowled until it looked like his face was going to implode, tapped his cigarette twice, as if the ash would mark his territory, then popped out again.

"See?" she said.

"But I thought you hung out with him."

"No, I don't hang out with him. He's just sort of laid claim to me. If I tell him to go away, he comes by my place and won't leave. A while back, he lured me in by giving me money to gamble." She pronounced the word "gamble" *gombil*, like something sacred. "He even took me to Puerto Rico so I could gombil. He's the devil." A shudder ran through her, and we sat there in silence while she puffed on her Marlboro Light and poked at the machine until it played the "Hallelujah Chorus" again.

"No one around here will help me. They don't get the picture. I'm all alone, waiting for this creep to go nuts and kill me when he finally figures out that I'm not going to play his sick game."

I looked at her frail waif fingers poking at the machine, her waif hair and pale waif face.

"I'll help you," I said.

The next day, I had trouble finding her place. Even though she'd given me specific directions, I kept winding up in front of a tiny tarpaper hut at the dead end of an alley. After my third loop around the block, I pulled into the dead end and in my rearview noticed a Ford Probe driving slowly past the entrance. It was the waif's devil, his face red and imploding, one of his hands on the steering wheel and the other dangling down from the driver's window with a cigarette. Tap, tap.

As he drove off, I heard the waif's voice and then saw her emerge from the darkness and tarpaper.

"Is he still there?" she said.

"No," I said, "I don't think so."

"He'll be back."

I saw more and more of the waif and the imploding red face and dangling cigarette over the next few months and started to realize that the waif was right, the man was a serious threat to her, himself and anyone who came between them, but oddly enough, I found the whole equation attractive, even exhilarating. My life seemed to have a purpose other than messing up the lives of others. I would help the waif out, and if I got killed in the process, so what.

But the equation wasn't quite that simple. For one thing, the waif was complex. A Teilhard de Chardin Catholic with a degree in philosophy, she would throw a towel over the statue of Jesus at the foot of her bed on the few occasions that I slept with her. Sometimes she even seemed demonic, and in an almost mythic transformation where her pale vulnerability changed to a dark, sanguine beauty, she would stomp around her little tarpaper empire splashing everything, including me, with holy water that came in a vial from Lourdes, screaming, "Go home to your wife. Your divorce is just a paper thing. You're using me like a whore. That's why you stay with me, isn't it? The ol' virgin/whore paradigm." This was the Bull-Waif.

For another thing, she surprised me with the effect she had on men in general. The second or third time I visited her, I had brought her coffee and was sitting at her card table while she flopped out my future in tarot cards, when someone knocked at her door. It was the local locksmith bringing her coffee. He looked something like me, and he blushed and stared at his feet when he saw that she was flopping out her cards for someone who looked like him. Another time, I was even more surprised when the Hollywood literary agent for some of the area's most famous writers showed up at the door with a bouquet of flowers. He seemed equally surprised to see me in what he had thought was his place at her tarot table.

She was also a transient. Before she settled in her tarpaper hut, she had lived out of cars and vans along the Yellowstone. Some of this time she spent near Gardiner with a wounded Vietnam vet named Moon Cookie, and some of it she lived alone in her car—until a group of teenage boys tried to stone her where she was parked across from Mayor's Landing on the Yellowstone near Livingston. Occasionally, to get out from under the puffy red eyes of her devil, I'd drive her out a couple of miles to the river, where I'd go through the numb motions of fishing and she'd stare hollow-eyed into the dark night of her soul and talk about St. John of the Cross until she'd recognize the van of a fellow transient passing or pulling in down the way and say, "That must be Billy" or "That looks like Michael's van. He's kind of a sociopath. We should leave."

Another glitch in the equation was that her devil, Mr. Probe, would upon occasion get out of his Probe and break into her house. This became apparent one day when the waif was cleaning and found a little sound-activated tape recorder intermittently whirring away under her bed. This sent her into Bull-Waif mode and eventually led us to the Park County Courthouse, where I sat in the hall with the locksmith as a reserve witness while the waif, her pro bono lawyer and a counselor from the women's shelter battled Mr. Probe and his lawyer (a woman well-respected in the community) to get a restraining order.

After many tears and much trauma, the waif got her restraining order, but it didn't do much good. When Mr. Probe sensed the presence of police near the waif's hut, he just expanded his range and drove over the hill to stalk me. When I'd walk down the hill from my classes, there'd be the Probe, the arm, the cigarette—tap, tap. When I'd go to stay with Judy, there'd be the Probe parked down the street—tap, tap. He took my briefcase from my truck where I'd left it and threw it in Bozeman Creek. He called Judy at all hours of the night, hanging up when she answered. He left notes about me and the waif in Judy's door and mailbox.

One night I surprised him by sneaking up on his Probe, opening the passenger's door and plopping down on the seat beside him. The interior smelled like a struck match and was filled with mashed down blankets and fast food wrappers from his dedicated life of stalking.

When he looked at me, I didn't see anger or even obsession —just a look of sorrow similar to the one I had been seeing on Judy's face.

"Why are you doing this?" I said.

"It's all I have left."

"What do you mean?" I said. "You have a family. You're a writer and an international traveler. People really like your book on trout fishing in Argentina." After I said that, I felt foolish because I knew exactly what he meant. Nothing means anything when there's a hole where your heart used to be.

"You do what you have to do," said Mr. Probe.

"Are you talking about me or about yourself?" I said.

"Does it matter?"

"No," I said, "I guess not." I got out of his Probe, and he drove off slowly with his arm out his side window, tapping his cigarette.

A few weeks later when he called and I met him at JB's Big Boy, he told me that he'd had a cocked and loaded .357 magnum under his seat while he was talking to me and that, a month earlier, after I'd moved from my Livingston house to the Murray Hotel, he had tried to poison me.

"Did you know that you almost accidentally poisoned Judy?" I said.

"I knew that was a possibility."

"You know I'll have to report this to the police."

"Of course you will, but that's okay because I'm pretty much finished."

"With what?" I said.

"I have to get out of here," he said, and he paid the tab for our coffee and left.

After I heard that he had broken his neck and died instantly when he drove off the overpass on the old highway east of Manhattan while trying to outrun the Highway Patrol, I felt almost as much relief for him as I did for Judy and the waif.

The waif eventually moved to Cleveland, Ohio, to be near her aging parents, and the last I heard, she had married a kind man who doesn't mind if, once in a while, she goes gambling with her sister or mother.

A Broken Toaster

. . . .

It's a gray February outside and Judy is bonking my head on the kitchen floor. Bonk, bonk, bonk, bonk. I can't tell if the tears on my face are mine or hers. She has a knee on each side of me and an ear in each hand. Bonk, bonk, bonk, bonk. I'm not doing anything to stop her because I know how she feels. On the one hand, her chronic bladder disease has been making her feel as if her lower abdomen is filled with razor blades. On the other hand, her husband has gone on the fritz like a faulty appliance—say, a toaster. For years the toaster has worked the way it's supposed to. You put in the bread, you push down the handle, you wait a couple of minutes and before you know it, pop, there's your toast. But then one day you press down the handle and the bread comes right back up, or, even worse, it stays down and turns all black and funny. That's when you give it a couple of gentle raps on the side. With luck, that'll do the trick. If not, you start banging the toaster against the kitchen floor.

In this case, since I'm Judy's toaster and I haven't responded to her gentle raps, she's resorted to these more desperate measures in hopes that she might realign my jumbled circuitry. Unlike a toaster, I'm with her all the way—at least for the moment, and because of said jumbled circuitry, for the moment is about all I can handle. We have tried other things—like marriage counselors.

The first one was sort of a cross between Bob Newhart and a basketball coach. He paced energetically back and forth before us, occasionally pounding his palm with his fist for emphasis, saying things like, "Greg, the ball's in your court," or "Judy, it might be your turn to take a time out while Greg goes one-on-one with his inner wise man." After about ten minutes of this, he looked at us both expectantly and said, "I don't want this to just be a one-way kind of deal. If you have any questions about what we're doing here, now's the time to ask them."

"Okay," said Judy, "why don't you just cut the fucking sports metaphors?"

"What?" said Dr. Newhart. This play was obviously not in his game plan.

"We're here because he's going nuts and I don't particularly want to be alive," said Judy, "and you're acting like this is a fucking game of basketball."

The next one was a smart, funny woman. Judy particularly liked her approach because she started out our session by saying, "The world would be a whole lot better place if all the men had their balls cut off and put in a big stew." I nodded my head in agreement, but I was thinking things like, "Big balls = bad toaster," and "Me want Bunny Girl." We stuck with this counselor for a while because she seemed to make Judy happy, but we eventually stopped seeing her when she and Judy realized that I was lying to both of them.

That was pretty much it for marriage counselors. What we finally settled on was a full-blown psychiatrist. Judy went to him first because I had just torn myself from her arms and run bleary-eyed into the Taylor-Hilgard wilderness to meet Bunny Girl and offer myself up to the grizzlies as a side dish to a gutted packhorse. For Judy, it was a coin-toss between killing herself and going to a psychiatrist. Fortunately, the latter won out. It made little difference that the psychiatrist she chose had been raked over the coals on *Sixty Minutes* for billing each separate personality of a client with a multiple personality disorder because he did what all good psychiatrists do. He told her what was wrong with her and prescribed some pills.

"You have separation anxiety disorder. Here, some of

these should calm you down. What's the matter with your husband?"

"I don't know. He keeps running away to see this girl, then he comes back to me all upset and crying."

"He has attention deficit disorder. Send him in and we'll fix him right up."

When Judy decided that she wasn't going to kill herself, she stopped going to the psychiatrist. As for the toaster, it took a couple of years, but with the help of Dr. Fix-It and a few thousand milligrams of amphetamine salt tablets, the circuitry gradually kicked back in. Twelve years later, it's still going to Dr. Fix-It for its amphetamine salt tablets.

Down from
Hellroaring

. . . .

Interstitial cystitis is one of those terrible diseases that you
never hear about until you get it, and then no one can empa-
thize because they've never heard of it. It basically happens
when the inside of your bladder cracks like an old inner tube
so there's nothing to protect the tissue from the urine, and
that whole part of your body stays inflamed for months—then
years, with only occasional letups. The person who has it feels
like they're in hell, and the person with the one who has it feels
totally helpless and, eventually, responsible.

When a woman has this disease, she needs all the support
she can get from her husband because nothing appears to be
wrong with her on the surface, and most people, even her
friends, either think she's faking it for attention and roll their
eyes when she goes on and on about the pain, or they understand the pain and stop seeing her because they don't want to
think about it. When a woman is in this state and her husband
abandons her and goes spinning off into a midlife crisis—well,
you get the picture.

I watched myself do this thing in horror and watched Judy
trying to deal with it in even more horror. A couple of times she
managed to dress herself up and go out looking for a man who
wouldn't leave her. Once she numbed herself with Vicodin,
went to the Bozeman Mall, and tried to make friends with a
furniture salesman. He was a Republican fundamentalist, the
antithesis of everything she believed in, but she didn't care

about that any more. He turned out to be a kind man, and married, and talked her into going back home.

On another occasion she went on a canoe trip with a man we had known from Bozeman's liberal community. Also on the trip was a potter who had gotten a divorce a few years before, his new young wife and her daughters from a previous marriage. Judy liked the man she was with and he liked her, but the potter kept putting his arms around his new wife and daughters and saying things like, "Look at the lucky old man, surrounded by young blondes," while, through her fog of painkillers, she was thinking, "Look at the disease-riddled old Bunny, ditched for a young blonde."

She didn't want to be with anyone but me. Her insides might have been twisted all funny, but her monogamous brain was painfully intact, and even though my state was the reverse of hers, her strength still brought me to tears when, one July afternoon, Jon Anderson and I came walking down the steep switchbacks off Hellroaring Creek and she was sitting at the foot of a huge boulder, out there in the middle of nowhere with lupine in her hair.

And again in the fall of that same year, I walked into the house and saw her standing in the living room holding a fly rod and wearing a pair of waders. Beside her on the coffee table was *A Complete Idiot's Guide to Fly-Fishing*. I got choked up and had to turn my head away when she said, "Will you take me fishing?" We stood together in the riffles just downstream from Williams Bridge as the sun set on the Gallatin that evening, and I held her in my arms as she made some short casts and caught a big pretty rainbow trout. Up until then I hadn't truly realized the depth of her despair. I had driven her to fish.

A Pile of Leaves

. . . .

In the fall of 1998, I was standing in my backyard staring glumly at a pile of leaves that I had just raked. I was living with Judy, who was letting me call her The Bunny again, in the little house where we had raised our boys. I was still having trouble with fishing; thus, when Judy was out of pain, the Queen was having trouble making her trips to Dondore, what with me short-circuiting her fantasies by wandering around the house and yard glumly staring at things.

I had learned to sit Dick down and give him a good talking to whenever he started to get out of hand, but my favorite fishing spots were still slightly tarnished from the old lies and excuses. As I stared at the pile of leaves, a voice came over the fence next to me.

"Nice-looking pile of leaves you've got there." It was Bill Moeckel, who had been my neighbor for sixteen years.

"I'm not sure what to do," I said.

"With the leaves?" said Bill.

"With the leaves, with myself, you name it."

"You look like you could use some surrogate daughters for fishing buddies," said Bill.

And that is how I started to be able to fish again. Bill and his wife Julie had been raising their daughters, Tessa and Tory, next door for years, and now they wanted to go fishing. This was new to me: kids who actually wanted to fish—and daughters to boot.

Tessa, the older one, was always a little apprehensive about it. Even after I put her on a spot on the lower Gallatin where she pulled out a big brown trout, she watched in horror as it flopped on the grass in front of her.

"Is it feeling any pain?" said Tessa, dropping her rod and staring at the fish.

"Sheer absolute horror and panic," said Bill, who has always had a knack for teasing his girls.

"Here, I'll put it to sleep," I said, whacking its head with a beaver-chewed stick.

"Noooo," said Tessa.

"Yummy," said Tory.

Eventually, the imagery of writhing worms and gutted trout distanced Tessa from the sport so that she and Judy would sit up on the bank reading and occasionally rolling their eyes as Tory, Julie, Bill and I went whooping up and down various shores, catching and subduing fish. Though Tessa eventually became a vegetarian and decided against fishing, I like to think that I had some influence on her becoming an English major at the University of Montana and more recently a talented poet.

Tory, on the other hand, took to fishing in much the same way I did. I sat her down by one of my favorite holes near the headwaters of the Missouri and showed her a few basics, hoping that she would catch a couple of small ones. Within five minutes, I looked down the bank and she was reeling in a two-pound rainbow trout.

"I've got one," said Tory.

"OK, now," I said, "it's a good one, so don't horse it. Keep your rod tip up."

But I hadn't finished my futile instructions before the fish was flopping on the bank and Tory was casting out again.

"This is easy," said Tory.

"No," I said, "it's not easy. You were just lucky. You need skill and patien . . ."

"I've got another one," said Tory, methodically reeling in a trout even larger than the previous one.

This went on until she caught her limit. Actually, it has pretty much gone on through high school, though she has been temporarily distracted from the lakes and rivers by her talents for painting and drumming.

Retied

. . . .

In the summer of 2000, The Bunny married me again, and I got my soul back. The Moeckels came down to the Gallatin County Law and Justice Center as our witnesses, and as Tory made faces and Tessa took pictures, Bill and Julie stood by as witnesses while Wanda, a court clerk, retied the knot.

After the ceremony, I sang Judy these lyrics I had written a few years earlier, when things were at their worst. It's a poem that my Sea Widow found among her husband's books and maps after he drowned at sea.

The Fisherman's Song

Long ago I heard it said
That love is like a river,
Reflecting while the rose is red,
Reflecting while it withers.

So pardon me my careless years
When I changed like the weather
And lost you like the rapids lose
Reflections on a river.

What use to tear this heart in two,
This heart that belongs to you.
Our life, this love are all I choose
On this morning of forever.

For years I sailed the wilderness
Searching for the answers

To questions that I did not know,
Taking foolish chances.

Can a mountain let her valley go?
Can a valley lose her river?
My fear and pain cried, "I don't know."
My true heart answered, "Never."

So sleep and close your sad gray eyes,
For I can't tell me from you.
I'll kiss them open when you rise
On this morning of forever.

I am fishing again, but not with the old urgency. I have taken to releasing fish much of the time so that my guide friends might stay in business, psychologists on two-week fishing vacations might have a quality experience and the wealthy people who have bought up much of the riverbanks to trout-fish might get their money's worth—though occasionally I'll go out with a friend or my neighbors and whack a couple for old time's sake.

I met Chris Schaberg, a graduate student in my department who reminds me of myself at his age in the way he approaches fishing more as a life function than as a sport. When he calls, he will not say, "Do you want to go fishing?" Instead, he will say, "Whippy sticks or sucker," which in our code means fly-fishing or bait fishing. He approaches life in much the same way, embracing the American West both for its pristine settings and its McDonald's franchises, and when we come upon a chunk of Styrofoam lodged in a logjam on the Gallatin, he will say, "Look, Nature!" in much the same way that Gary Snyder now includes McDonald's and Motel Six in the landscapes of his more recent poetry.

And though David Behr followed The Bunny's example,

stopped holding his breath and gave up on my ESPN career, he has started a website called "Troutball" where he posts my various failed attempts at fishing fame, along with pictures of gargantuan carp caught on flies by his friend Tony, alias Gill Finn. There, one may also find a link to the Temple of the Weeping Sucker.

David has even hired me as a sort of Troutball mascot and has flown me down to the Aspen area to play silly fishing songs for the Whitefish Roundup, an event in which guides compete to catch the most and largest whitefish. Twice, David, Tony and I have hauled a leaky trailer loaded with coolers full of over four hundred iced-down whitefish to the Denver Rescue Mission, where they were cooked up as meals for the down and out.

And sometimes in the spring, when the rivers are too high and muddy for fishing, I'll leave my rod at home and hunt morel, bolete, oyster or chanterelle mushrooms with friends like Michael Sexson, Doug Peacock, Dan Sullivan, Sid Gustafson, Greg Owens or Mike Devine. In this endeavor, we may still hear the rush of a stream, smell the pines and watch the ouzels, ospreys and kingfishers, but we temporarily abandon the old dilemmas concerning the proper method of obtaining our prey and whether or not it should be released.

As I sit here in Judy's room typing this on a cool, sunny day in April 2007 in Bozeman, Montana, I have no immediate plans to go fishing, though I may change my mind. I think of The Bunny, who has rented an apartment in Washington, D.C., for three months to help Max's wife Perrin with our new grandson Henry and our even newer granddaughter, Charlotte. Max and Chris both have jobs there, and I know that they are taking good care of their mother. If Henry and Charlotte ever want to fish, I'll try to be as good a partner as Granddad was. If not, I'll be just as happy if they watch me come and go with detached bemusement—or, even better, take me by my old, warty hand and lead me in some new direction.

Fate has added diabetes and sarcoidosis to Judy's interstitial cystitis, but she keeps going, rolling her eyes, not holding her breath, taking the occasional pilgrimage to Dondore and giving me her permission to fish. I called her last night and she said the cherry blossoms on the Potomac are in full bloom. Just after they fall, she will be coming home to me.

Now I think of a boat on Long Lake, a boat on Lake Tenkiller, a boat on the Bosporus, a boat on the Mediterranean, a boat near the Golden Gate, a boat on a Natchitoches bayou; of family and friends long dead and still alive; of Minnesota, Oklahoma, New York, Turkey, Idaho, California, Louisiana and now Montana. I think of a river darkening into its folds with the blues and reds of a sunset, how it flows beyond knowledge and all these forlorn rags of growing old, and I think of Judy, the Bunny I've always had. I think of The Bunny.